T0343037

B2 FIRST

WORKBOOK WITHOUT ANSWERS

with Audio Download

Claire Wijayatilake

Cambridge University Press
www.cambridge.org/elt

Cambridge Assessment English
www.cambridgeenglish.org

Information on this title: www.cambridge.org/9781108647861

© Cambridge University Press & Assessment and UCLES 2019

First published 2019

20 19 18 17 16 15 14 13

Printed in Dubai by Oriental Press

A catalogue record for this publication is available from the British Library

ISBN 978-1-108-64786-1 Workbook without answers with Audio Download

CONTENTS

S LET'S TALK

GRAMMAR

1 Put the verb in brackets at the end of each sentence into the past simple, present perfect simple or present perfect continuous.

1 _____ you ever _____ someone from another country? (*meet*)
2 My cousins _____ since January. They're due home next week. (*travel*)
3 I _____ Jack the other day. He's working as a teacher in our local secondary school. (*see*)
4 I _____ never _____ bungee jumping but I hope to one day. (*try*)
5 You look exhausted. What _____ you _____? (*do*)
6 I _____ to their new album yet. Is it any good? (*listen*)
7 Dominic _____ French and German when he was at school. (*study*)
8 I _____ Ella for about ten years. (*know*)
9 I _____ her an email two weeks ago and she still _____ . (*send*) (*reply*)
10 Someone _____ my dinner! Half of it is missing. (*eat*)

2 Complete the sentences with the comparative or superlative form of the adjective in brackets.

1 In my opinion, English is _____ (easy) to learn than French.
2 This is _____ (good) film I have ever seen!
3 She is _____ (confident) in using technology than I am. I'm hopeless!
4 Tom is _____ (tall) Max. They're both 1.74 m.
5 It feels _____ (hot) today than it was yesterday.
6 That was _____ (relaxing) holiday I have ever been on.
7 I thought the second series was _____ (bad) than the first.
8 New York and London are both wonderful cities but Madrid is _____ (beautiful) of the three, in my opinion.

VOCABULARY

Match the speakers (1–5) with the most appropriate adjective in the box.

annoyed	delighted	disappointed	shocked	worried

1 I actually passed. I'm so happy because I worked really hard for these exams and now I can go to the university I really wanted!

2 I've been waiting here for almost two hours. I'm now late for my next seminar and all I wanted to do was get a signature for this document.

3 Did you see the series finale!? I still can't believe how it ended. I really didn't see that coming, to be honest.

4 I'm really nervous about my driving test next week. I've practised a lot but I still don't think I'm ready for it.

5 I know I didn't do too well in the interview, but I thought they might still offer me the job. It's sad but I will continue to apply for other roles.

LISTENING

02 You will hear five learners of English talking about difficulties they have faced with communication. For each speaker, choose a problem A–H. There are three letters you do not need to use.

1 Speaker 1 ....
2 Speaker 2 ....
3 Speaker 3 ....
4 Speaker 4 ....
5 Speaker 5 ....

A The speaker found British English difficult to understand.

B The speaker did the wrong kind of preparation for his/her overseas trip.

C The speaker's classmates were not interested in learning.

D The speaker had not studied much grammar before.

E The speaker lacked confidence because he felt his/her English was not perfect.

F The speaker relied too heavily on translation from his/her mother tongue.

G The speaker's teacher was too strict.

H The speaker mixes up different varieties of English.

WRITING

Read this story about a girl called Anya, whose family gave up communication technology for a month. Complete each gap with a word or phrase from the box.

| anyway | as long as | as you can imagine | in theory |
| looking back | not even | on the bright side | secretly |

Two years ago, when I was 14, my parents decided to sign our family up for an experiment which would be made into a reality TV series. What we would have to do is survive for a whole month without access to our usual communication devices. We would have no phones – **(1)** .... a landline – no radio, TV or computers. It was during the summer holidays so, **(2)** .... , there was no reason why we couldn't live without those things – there was no homework to do for school. We could go to the local shop and we were allowed to buy a newspaper every day. Books were allowed, but not magazines.

I was not that keen on taking part, but **(3)** .... I was hoping I would be talent-spotted and it would lead to a brilliant career in television. My older brother, Marcus, was not that bothered as all he ever did was read books **(4)** .... My sister, Molly, was too young to care. **(5)** .... she had her toys and her pet rabbit to play with she was fine. Mum and Dad were always telling me to 'get off that phone!' and they were the ones who applied to take part.

Anyway, **(6)** .... , it was quite a challenge for me! I was so used to googling everything that came into my head, playing games on my phone for hours and chatting to my friends that being without technology was like losing a part of my body. **(7)** .... , the weather was great that summer so I spent a lot of time outside. I took up running and got really fit. I cycled over to my friends' houses as I couldn't call them to meet up in town. I read about five novels and really enjoyed the feel of an actual book in my hand. So, **(8)** .... , it was not as bad as I had expected. Would I want to live like that all the time? Definitely not!

READING

Read the article. Complete Exercises 1 and 2 on page 7.

Artificial intelligence and language learning

As a language student, you have probably used artificial intelligence in numerous ways. You may have taken an adaptive placement test to join your class or practised your grammar with the help of an online learning platform. However, you have probably felt the limitations of relying solely on technology for feedback on your progress, particularly when it comes to the productive skills of speaking and writing. How far can a computer help you with those?

If you are studying English – or any other language – in a class with a teacher, the chances are you have been asked to give a presentation to the rest of the class. It is also likely that the presentations you have given have been followed by feedback, first from the other students and then from your teacher. Hopefully, this was a positive experience for you. However, you may have felt that the feedback was either inaccurate or too subjective. Perhaps your classmates did not want you to feel bad, so they said you were amazing, or you did not agree with your teacher that you 'failed to engage your audience'. What if there were a computer programme that could give you a completely objective reaction to your presentation? How would it work and would you trust it?

When we give a presentation – whether in business, in class or for some other purpose – we always hope for a positive reaction from those listening to us. We want our audience to really listen, trust us, engage with us and act on what we have said in some way – maybe to change their way of thinking or to buy our product. Extensive research has helped us understand the ways in which speakers can influence an audience's reaction to them. These include the content of our talk, our body language and how we use our words and voices. Machines can now be trained to measure these factors and give us objective feedback to help us improve our communication skills. One business coach who uses this kind of software to teach presentation skills says: 'Giving feedback with the use of technology is much less personal. You can't argue with a computer!'

Some exam boards have already started to use artificial intelligence to mark students' written work. Hundreds or even thousands of essays scored by teachers are fed into the computer, which learns to recognise the features of an essay with a particular score. Some studies have shown this to be more accurate than human marking because it eliminates human failings such as tiredness and personal preferences. However, the whole concept horrifies many working in the classroom. Teacher and writer Bill Walsh states that, 'At the very least, writing requires a breathing reader.'

The nature of artificial intelligence is that the more data you provide, the better it works. This means that as time passes and more data is added, the more we will be able to rely on it to give us feedback on our performance. One of Walsh's objections to computers marking essays is that they will not be able to recognise humour, irony, originality of expression or the very subtle differences in meaning between two words. That may be true at present, but with enough data to work with and the right training, who knows what they might be capable of?

Although performing tasks with the use of artificial intelligence is faster, more cost effective and in many ways more accurate, there are some limitations of artificial intelligence which seem impossible to overcome. Computers are not able to empathise, they do not possess self-awareness and they are poor at multitasking. A teacher will be aware that the local football team lost an important match or that students have been delayed in a traffic jam. He or she has access to up-to-the-minute information from a range of sources – and a lifetime of experience in how to react to different situations and different personality types. Artificial intelligence can definitely help teachers, but I think they can rest assured that their jobs are safe for a few more years.

1 **Which attitudes (A–F) are expressed by the writer?**

A Presentation feedback given by humans is better than that given by computers.

B Professional trainers find computers useful in supporting their feedback to learners.

C Computers are unlikely to get better at marking essays.

D The drawbacks of artificial intelligence are very significant.

E Computers will soon be able to understand human emotions.

F Computers are likely to replace teachers in the near future.

2 **Choose the correct option in each sentence.**

1 Computers are more useful when you are practising *receptive* / productive*** skills.

2 Feedback from computers can be more *objective / subjective* than feedback from other students.

3 The third paragraph is generally *for / against* the use of artificial intelligence in presentation feedback.

4 According to the text, teachers *like / dislike* the idea of using artificial intelligence to mark essays.

5 Bill Walsh believes that computers *will / will not* be able to recognise sophisticated language.

6 The final paragraph emphasises the *similarities / differences* between teachers and computers.

*reading and listening

**writing and speaking

SPEAKING

 03 **You will hear eight students answering one question each. Match the speakers (1–8) to the questions they were asked (A–H).**

1 ....

2 ....

3 ....

4 ....

5 ....

6 ....

7 ....

8 ....

A Have you ever collected anything?

B Is there anyone in your family who inspires you?

C How long have you lived in your hometown?

D When did you last go out with your friends?

E Which member of your family are you most similar to?

F What kind of things do you usually do with your friends?

G What sport or hobby would you like to try?

H What do you like about your hometown?

1 FIGHTING FIT

GRAMMAR

1 **Tick the correct sentences. Correct those which contain an error.**

1 I refuse joining a gym – it's too expensive!

2 Serge dislikes playing any kind of team game.

3 Olympic athletes start training at a very early age.

4 I've given up horse riding. I can't risk to fall off at my age!

5 Stop to play on the ice! It might break.

6 Have you managed to lose any weight yet?

7 Many people avoid to eat a lot of red meat.

2 **Match the parts of the sentences.**

1	Is this exercise supposed	**A**	going to the cinema or the gym?
2	Saira regrets	**B**	eating meals after 8pm.
3	The food in Japan tends	**C**	to eat five portions of fruit or vegetables a day.
4	Are you still able	**D**	not to eat any more sweets!
5	Do you prefer	**E**	to be healthier than in other countries.
6	Everyone should aim	**F**	to touch your toes?
7	You should stop	**G**	to hurt this much?
8	Yes, doctor, I promise	**H**	eating junk food when she was young.

3 Choose the correct option in these sentences.

1 Everyone knows that fruit juice contains a lot of sugar. *Although / Nevertheless*, many people let their children drink it every day.

2 *Instead of / While* snacking on biscuits and cake, eat a handful of nuts and seeds. It's much healthier.

3 *Despite / Even though* the bad weather, they went ahead with the race.

4 *In spite of / Although* he was in pain, Fabio finished the marathon.

5 It can be challenging to follow a healthy diet. *However / Whereas*, it is worth it in the long run.

6 You should go for a walk after dinner *despite / rather than* sitting on the sofa and watching TV.

4 Read this extract from an email a woman has written to her local government representative. Fill in the gaps with the linking words and phrases from the box. Add capital letters to the words if necessary.

whereas	despite	however	instead of
although	unlike	in the past	

•●● ◀▶   🔍 🏠
                              Reply Forward ✉

I am a local resident concerned about the health of our children. I don't think local government is doing enough to protect the younger generation. **(1)** _____ the fact that the government recommends children eat healthy food, there are eight or nine fast food restaurants in our town!
(2) _____, there are still no restaurants which focus on home-cooked, healthy meals at affordable prices. Another problem is the lack of exercise facilities. **(3)** _____ there are several gyms, they are not open to children under the age of 16. **(4)** _____ making these facilities available to adults only, gyms could be encouraged to welcome children at certain times. Our local parks used to be a great place for children to play sports with their friends. **(5)** _____, they are not being maintained properly so it is not a good environment for them. There used to be a team of gardeners and maintenance staff, **(6)** _____ now there is only one person looking after all the parks.
I suggest we make improvements to our town to give our children a healthier future.

Complete the second sentence with a phrase from Unit 1 of the Student's book so that it has a similar meaning to the first sentence. Use between two and five words for each sentence, including the word in bold.

1 It is important to monitor how you're doing.
KEEP
Always try to _____ your progress.

2 Unfortunately, I just couldn't run as fast as them.
KEEP
Unfortunately, I just couldn't _____ them.

3 You should try to reduce the amount of sugar in your diet.
DOWN
It is a good idea to _____ on sugar.

4 We weren't sure whether our team would win.
TOUCH
It was _____ whether our team would win.

5 I stay fit by running three times a week.
SHAPE
I _____ by running three times a week.

PUSH YOURSELF C1

_____ .

Read the sentences and use the context to match the underlined words to their meanings.

1 I am interested in taking a course in nutrition as I think we all need to watch what we eat.

2 If you are going to run a marathon, you need to improve your stamina.

3 It is important to eat plenty of fruit and vegetables to help your digestion.

4 If you have bad posture, you can suffer from back problems.

5 I think it is important to find a form of exercise that combines both physical and mental well-being.

A Health and happiness

B Food and the effect it has on health

C The process in which the body breaks down food

D The ability to keep going for a long time

E The way someone sits, stands or holds themselves

Read this article about fitness activities and match questions 1–10 on page 11 with letters A–D.

UNUSUAL
FITNESS ACTIVITIES

A Hot yoga

Yoga has long been considered one of the best exercises around, and one that can be practised virtually anywhere, including at home. Hot yoga, as the name suggests, takes it a stage further by turning up the heat, requiring a temperature of around 40° C and humidity of 60 per cent. Clearly, such a change is going to make you sweat more, and this is the whole point as it is supposed to eliminate harmful chemicals and toxins from your body. In a nutshell, hot yoga retains the mental focus of the more traditional version of the discipline but is designed to push your body much harder. The heat increases your heart rate and helps thin the blood, stimulate your metabolism and burn calories at a faster rate. As well as increased strength, stamina and flexibility, practitioners point to a number of other health benefits, such as curing back pain and improving the skin, with many even claiming it has boosted their performance in other sports.

B Aerial fitness

If you ever went to the circus as a child, you probably marvelled at the power and fitness of aerial performers. So if you have ever thought of having a go at such activities yourself, aerial fitness, which is based on similar techniques, may be just what you are looking for. Learners usually start off with the silks – two lengths of fabric attached to the ceiling. Once you have mastered some climbs, you then practise various ways of manoeuvring the body around them, including learning to hang upside down – not something you do every day! More expert practitioners can later progress to more complex devices, such as hoops, trapezes and slings, and there is even an aerial form of yoga that you can try. Aerial fitness techniques do require you to support your own body weight so clearly the benefits include improved general strength and also increased shoulder mobility. Furthermore, think of the respect you will get from friends and family when you tell them all about it!

C Underwater cycling

Underwater cycling or aqua-cycling combines the concept of a spinning class with the benefits of exercising in water. For those new to the concept, it does literally mean that exercise bicycles are placed in a swimming pool! While spinning, which often involves standing up and bouncing, can create strain on your knees, cycling underwater prevents stress on the joints, because the water provides extra support for the body. Unlike spinning too, it is suitable for people of any age, size or shape, even pregnant women and those recovering from injuries, making it perfect for those who find the idea of group exercise a little intimidating.

D Obstacle races

If these were a favourite from your primary school sports day, you can now recreate the fun on a much grander scale. Obstacle races have become fashionable again and you are guaranteed to have a great time with your friends and family while keeping fit. These are usually large-scale, organised events, which can be in urban or rural settings and can involve all kinds of natural and man-made obstacles. You could be jumping over fires, climbing walls or crossing rivers. You might bounce on trampolines, slide down huge water chutes or crawl through tunnels. One thing you can be sure of is that there will be mud – lots of mud! The race might involve dressing up in silly costumes and will probably end with a giant party. Check the internet for events coming up near you.

Which activity

is mentioned as being good for impressing others?	**1** ....
is described as a bigger version of a competitive event from childhood?	**2** ....
is claimed to help remove damaging substances from your body?	**3** ....
uses a change of environment to make it less stressful on the body?	**4** ....
sees beginners learn to adopt an uncommon body position?	**5** ....
is an intentionally more challenging version of a well-known activity?	**6** ....
would be fun for anyone who participates, in the writer's opinion?	**7** ....
allows users to move on to different equipment as they improve?	**8** ....
is claimed to help athletes do better in other sporting disciplines?	**9** ....
is appropriate for those who don't necessarily have good levels of fitness?	**10** ....

SPEAKING PART 2

A

B

1 **Look at the photos and decide which photo (A or B) each comment corresponds to.**

1 It looks a lot riskier and more exciting than the other picture.

2 They can do whatever they want rather than doing what they're told to do.

3 It looks very controlled – everyone looks the same as everyone else.

4 Even though it looks a little boring, it's probably very good exercise.

5 One key difference is that they're out in the fresh air instead of being stuck inside a gym.

6 It looks as though they are at school or in a club.

7 I'd say the risk of injury is much greater.

2 **Choose the correct preposition in these sentences describing the photos.**

1 There are buildings *on / in* either side of the photo.

2 I can see some kind of gym equipment *in / at* the back of the photo.

3 The girls are standing *in / on* the tips of their toes.

4 Both boys are right *in / at* the middle of the photo.

5 There are some ropes hanging down *to / from* the ceiling.

6 I can see blue sky *on / in* the background.

7 *In / On* the top left corner of the photo there are some ladders.

8 *On / In* the foreground there is a brick wall.

2 KEEPING IN TOUCH

GRAMMAR

1 🔊 04 **Listen to the conversation between Katie and Patrick, who have just started their first jobs after leaving university. Are the statements True or False?**

1 Patrick has fully adjusted to working life.
2 Katie is happy with her salary.
3 Patrick and Katie were short of money when they were students.
4 They waited a long time to get cheap theatre tickets.
5 Katie used to get up early for her university lectures.
6 Patrick finds it easier to get up for work than Katie does.
7 As students, Patrick and Katie had to dress smartly.
8 Patrick has always worn a tie.

2 **For each sentence, choose the correct form of the verb.**

1 In the past, people didn't *used / use* to lock their front doors when they went out.
2 When my parents arrived in Europe from Jamaica, they found it hard to get *use / used* to the cold.
3 I'm from a large family. I'm used to *share / sharing* a room.
4 In my town, people used to *putting / put* their babies out in the garden all morning. I'm glad they don't do that anymore!
5 Families *used / use* to be much larger – having seven or eight children was quite normal.
6 Society is gradually *being / getting* used to the idea of men staying at home to bring up children while their wives go out to work.
7 *Were / Did* you use to cycle to school?
8 I *do / am* not used to walking so much. I usually drive everywhere.

3 **Why do you think each speaker decided to use the passive? Choose the correct options. For some sentences, both may be possible.**

1 My parents' house was broken into a couple of years ago.
   A The speaker doesn't know who did the action.
   B It's not important who did the action.
2 Flour is sieved and added to the mixture.
   A To show that it is a formal situation.
   B To describe a process.
3 Manchester United were knocked out in the first round by Liverpool.
   A The speaker doesn't know who did the action.
   B The speaker is mainly focused on Manchester United.
4 Milk used to be delivered to almost every house in England.
   A Because we already know that milkmen deliver milk.
   B Because this is no longer true.
5 *A Christmas Carol* was written by Charles Dickens. It's the story of an unhappy man called Ebenezer Scrooge.
   A The speaker is focused on *A Christmas Carol*.
   B The speaker is focused on Charles Dickens.
6 I would like to inform you that your loan repayments have not been made for the last two months.
   A It's a formal situation.
   B The speaker wants to be indirect.

4 Can these sentences be changed to the passive voice? Write in the passive those that can be changed. Put a cross (X) next to those that cannot. There are two examples (A and B) to help you.

Examples

A My mum grew these tomatoes – *These tomatoes were grown by my mum.*

B The plane arrived at 15.35. ✗

1 Amesh cooked this delicious curry.

2 I think all the students will understand the lesson.

3 I belong to the local tennis club.

4 The teacher has told me off three times now.

5 Joachim first came to the United Kingdom in 2009.

6 When did they discover those ruins?

7 I slept through my alarm this morning.

8 They are going to make a new version of the film *Titanic*.

PUSH YOURSELF C1

Rewrite the sentences using hedging language. The first one has been done for you.

People have said that social media has had a negative impact on our lives.
It has been said that social media has had a negative impact on our lives.

1 People have suggested that online friends aren't real friends.

2 People argue that friendship is less sincere nowadays.

3 People have said that families are growing further apart.

4 People believe that social media will become less popular in the future.

VOCABULARY

1 Complete each gap with a word for a family relationship.

1 My brother has a son. He is my _____ .

2 Tim married Rosie, who already had a daughter called Chloe from a previous marriage. Chloe is Tim's _____ .

3 Ana is married to Claudio. Claudio's father is Santiago. Santiago is Ana's _____ .

4 My aunt Emilia has two children, a boy and a girl. They are my _____ .

5 My husband has a sister called Julia. Julia is my _____ .

6 My uncle Tobias died last year. He was married to Surekha, who is now his _____ .

7 I've got two _____ , one brother and one sister.

8 Alberto's daughter has a daughter called Sofia. Sofia is Alberto's _____ .

2 Match the questions to the answers.

1 Have you ever fallen out with a friend?

2 Do you get on well with the other students in your class?

3 Who do you take after in your family?

4 Who do you look up to in your family?

5 What do you get up to at weekends?

6 Have you ever met up with someone you met online?

A No, I'm not sure that would be a good idea.

B My dad, definitely. We're both tall with dark, curly hair.

C I usually hang out with my friends.

D Yes, I once stopped talking to Derek for a month!

E Yes, we often go out for a coffee together after the lesson.

F My older sister. She's a really brilliant student.

05 **You will hear an interview with psychologist Antonia Russo, who is talking about the influence of birth order on personality. For questions 1–7, choose the best answer (A, B or C).**

1 What led Dr Russo to become interested in birth order and personality?

   A her own two children

   B her childhood experiences

   C her role as a psychologist

2 One possible reason for the success of firstborn children is that

   A they get more attention from their parents.

   B they are naturally more gifted.

   C they tend to be more interested in creative activities.

3 According to Dr Russo, the youngest child may

   A have problems with their identity.

   B be lacking in self-confidence.

   C be good at getting their own way.

4 How did being the middle child affect Dr Russo?

   A She became very close to her sisters.

   B She didn't get noticed by her family.

   C She sometimes went against her parents.

5 What does Dr Russo say about only children?

   A They are generally the most spoilt.

   B They share similar characteristics to firstborns.

   C They are usually the best leaders.

6 What does Dr Russo think about the role that gender plays in influencing children's personalities?

   A She feels that not enough research has been done in this area.

   B She believes that parents need to consider this when raising their children.

   C She doubts whether it affects the way that children develop.

7 Dr Russo sums up by saying that

   A birth order strongly influences personality.

   B the development of personality is complex.

   C further studies on birth order are needed.

1 Look at the Writing Part 1 question.

In your English class you have watched a documentary about families with lots of children. Your teacher has asked you to write an essay giving your opinion on large families.

What are the advantages and disadvantages of being a member of a large family?

Notes

Write about:

1 having a ready-made social network

2 the problem of lacking space and privacy

3 … (your own idea)

Which opening paragraph (A, B or C) is the best as the start of an answer to the question?

A If you are part of a large family, you will have a ready-made social network. You are sure to get on well with at least some of your siblings. The problem would be if you didn't have a big enough house because you wouldn't get enough space to keep your things. You might be interrupted by your little brothers and sisters when you were trying to do your homework.

B In the past, it was common for families to have many children. Nowadays, though, the average in developed countries is between one and two children per family. However, there are some couples who choose not to follow this trend and have large numbers of children. What would it be like to be a child with many siblings?

C My opinion is that when it comes to families, it's a case of 'the bigger, the better'. I am from a family of six children myself and we do have lots of fun together. It teaches you to be less selfish and to be satisfied with less. It can be quite chaotic but I wouldn't have it any other way.

2 Read the rest of the essay. Complete the gaps with words or phrases from the box. Add capital letters to the words if necessary.

> for me   it doesn't matter whether   finally
> one of the main drawbacks   there is no doubt that

(1) .... children with many siblings are never lonely. They do not need to arrange to meet up with friends or join clubs because there is a ready-made social circle at home. Furthermore, small children will be cared for by older brothers and sisters as well as by their parents.

(2) .... of life in a big family would be the lack of space and privacy. It might be difficult to find a quiet spot to do your homework and it would not really be possible to invite friends round to such a crowded home. **(3)** ...., sharing a room with one or more siblings would be the worst part and I believe this would cancel out the positive aspects.

(4) ...., growing up in a large family develops positive characteristics. Children will not be spoilt by being given everything they want. They have to share and help others from an early age.

In my opinion, **(5)** .... your family is big or small. What matters is that it's a happy family.

3 BEYOND THE CLASSROOM

GRAMMAR

1 06 **Listen to a teacher giving advice to a student called Donny, who is planning to study medicine. Which pieces of advice does she mention?**

1 Find out how doctors work.
2 Use online resources to get information.
3 Don't worry about specialising yet.
4 You only need to do one work experience placement.
5 Make contact with students in a similar situation to yours.
6 Concentrate only on your studies.
7 Keep your career options open.
8 Start visiting universities you'd like to apply to.

PUSH YOURSELF C1

Read the conditional sentences. Choose the correct option (A, B or C) for each gap.

1 _____ sell you the answers to the exam, please let your teacher know immediately.
   A Was anyone try to
   B Were anyone to try
   C Should anyone try to

2 _____ by the university of your choice, I am sure you will be able to find another excellent one to go to.
   A Were you not be accepted
   B Should you not be accepted
   C Shouldn't you accepted

3 I would be very angry _____ that your homework was copied from another student.
   A should I to find out
   B were I finding out
   C were I to find out

4 _____ a student identity card, you won't be able to register with the library.
   A Should you not have
   B Were you not to have
   C Weren't you have

5 _____ a question during the exam, please raise your hand and wait for the examiner to come to your desk.
   A Were you have
   B Should you have
   C Should you not have

2 **Complete the sentences with the first or second conditional forms of the verbs in the box.**

learn	join	need	pass	quit	work

1 If I _____ my exam, I will be really happy.
2 I would _____ a gym if I didn't have classes all the time.
3 If you _____ hard, you won't be able to get the grades you want.
4 I _____ to play the guitar if I had the time.
5 You'll _____ to get a visa if you want to study in China.
6 I _____ my job if I could afford to.

3 **Complete the gaps with the correct form of the verb in brackets. There may be more than one possible answer.**

1 Provided he achieves his predicted grades, William _____ (start) college in September.
2 As soon as I _____ (finish) my homework, I'm going out to play football.
3 I will fail this exam unless a miracle _____ (happen)!
4 The school fun run will take place on Sunday, assuming it _____ (not rain).
5 What if someone _____ (offer) to do your assignment for you? Would you accept?
6 As long as everyone in the group _____ (do) what they're supposed to, we should win the best project award.
7 You _____ (be able to) enrol on that accountancy course unless you have passed your maths and economics exams.
8 Supposing you had to take the B2 First exam tomorrow, do you think you _____ (be) ready?

VOCABULARY

1 Complete the word families table. There may be more than one possible answer.

NOUN(S)	VERB(S)	ADJECTIVE(S)
experience	(1)	experiential
(2)	experiment	(3) ....
(4)	(5)	educational, educated
study, student	(6)	studious
(7)	graduate	graduate
tutor, tutorial	(8)	tutorial

2 Complete the sentences using words from the table. Change the form of the word if necessary.

1 Being a scientist means you often need to conduct ....
2 I attended my sister's .... ceremony yesterday. We were all so proud of her.
3 At university, you have different classes called lectures, seminars and ....
4 She has a lot of .... in medicine. She's been a doctor for 30 years.
5 Amina is a very .... girl. She is always reading books and never forgets her homework.
6 It is important to .... children about the importance of protecting the environment.

3 Match the sentences (1–7) with the idioms (A–G) that describe them.

1 I got 100 per cent in my recent English exam.
2 I stayed up all night in order to finish the project.
3 I love reading books about biology.
4 I worked for 10 hours more than I should have.
5 I memorised all the tenses in English.
6 I'm so happy about my exam result.
7 I am my teacher's favourite student.

A I am over the moon.
B I am the teacher's pet.
C I passed with flying colours.
D I pulled an all-nighter.
E I went the extra mile.
F I am a bookworm.
G I learned them by heart.

4 Complete the sentences with the words in the box. You may need to change the form of some of the words.

> a study   campus   cram   dissertation   graduation ceremony
> lecture theatre   resit   win a scholarship

1 I'm so happy that I've .... I don't think I would have been able to afford to go to university otherwise.
2 The university recently published .... which looks at the effects exams have on young learners.
3 Unfortunately, my sister has failed one of her exams so she needs .... it next month.
4 There's plenty of accommodation for students on .... , which means that we won't have far to go to get to our lectures every morning.
5 I submitted my .... yesterday. It came to a total of 15,000 words, which is by far the longest piece of writing I've ever had to do.
6 The .... will take place in the Hawking Building. Students are allowed to bring up to four guests.
7 Michelle won't be able to join us as she's busy .... for her English exam in two days.
8 The presentation on virtual learning will be held in the main .... and will last for approximately one hour.

You are going to read a magazine article about an innovative school in New York. Six sentences have been removed from it. Choose the missing sentence (A–G) that fits each gap (1–6). There is one sentence you don't need.

SCHOOLS OF THE FUTURE

Educational psychologist Neil Akidil visits a school with a modern approach to teaching and learning.

Although society has changed dramatically with the advent of information technology, education has not changed as much as might have been expected.

Classrooms now contain computers, but there is more that is the same about education now compared with 60 years ago than is different. **(1)** _____ A typical school day is divided into periods for different subjects, which are studied in isolation. There may be occasional projects, but these are often pushed to the sidelines and not allowed to get in the way of the 'real' work of completing the academic syllabus.

The Portfolio School in Tribeca, New York is different and may give us a glimpse into the schools of the future. **(2)** _____ This method is centred around an interdisciplinary model of learning, and project work is central to the approach. Children are not divided into grades by age and the school day is not divided into subjects.

Instead, the year is broken into 'learning units' lasting three or four months, each of which can be approached from a variety of angles. **(3)** _____ So, for example, in a lesson on colour, the students designed and made a lightbox projector and programmed an LED bonfire.

The Portfolio School has other differences from regular schools, too. There is no homework – research has shown it is not very useful. Teachers are not seen as the possessors of knowledge which they then pass on

to their students. **(4)** _____ According to the school, their approach causes deep learning to occur in children, fuelled by genuine curiosity rather than obligation. The philosophy of the school is based on preparing children for the actual world they will live in, which is technological, global and entrepreneurial. There is an emphasis on thinking skills and self-reflection, which are vital in the modern world.

The parents of children who attend the school are delighted with their children's progress. The system focuses on creating a need for learning, rather than teachers simply teaching facts from a pre-defined syllabus. **(5)** _____ However, at Portfolio, this soon changed. When the same child wanted to build a model, she quickly realised that in order to do so she needed to learn how to carry out certain measurements and calculations. Suddenly she had a motivation to learn maths and now, a few months on, she loves the subject. Her father points to his daughter's developing educational independence and says that these days she 'skips to school'.

The Portfolio School is, sadly, not accessible to everyone. **(6)** _____ However, the school is keen to reach out to the wider community and serve as a model of what education can be. The school may have world-class facilities, including 3D printers for the children to use, but they emphasise that these are just tools. It is the philosophy and approach that makes the school what it is. In theory, this could be replicated anywhere. So, the question is, will all schools look like Portfolio in the future?

A For example, one mother highlighted the fact that her daughter had struggled at maths at regular schools because of the lack of practical application of the subject.

B The annual fees of $35,000 are discouraging for the vast majority of parents and the student capacity of the school is limited.

C There are tests but children can take them any time they feel ready and they mark them themselves.

D The school's approach is research-based and has been developed by an impressive panel of experts in learning and child development.

E Students still generally sit in rows with a teacher at the front and the curriculum is specified in advance, usually by governments or local authorities.

F Rather, they are considered mentors who guide and assist the learners.

G The focus is always on creativity, design and practical learning.

SPEAKING PART 3

1 🎧 07 **Listen to two students, Mario and Yuriko, doing the first part of the Part 3 task below. For each factor shown, decide if they agree or disagree on how important it is.**

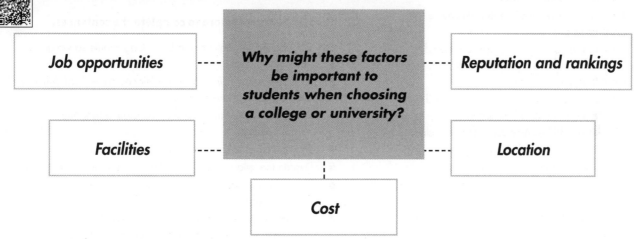

Job opportunities

Why might these factors be important to students when choosing a college or university?

Reputation and rankings

Facilities

Location

Cost

2 **Look at these expressions from the audio. Match them to their function (A–D).**

1 I'm afraid I completely disagree with you there.
2 I suppose you might be right.
3 I'd go along with that.
4 I'm not so sure about that.
5 It means …
6 I see your point.
7 I agree up to a point.
8 What I mean by that is …

A Showing agreement
B Showing disagreement
C Partial agreement/disagreement
D Giving clarification

3 🎧 08 **Now listen to the second part of the Part 3 task and choose True or False for each statement.**

		T	F
1	Mario thinks it is easy to decide which factor to choose.	T	F
2	Mario and Yuriko agree that location and cost are less important factors.	T	F
3	Mario believes that the principal motivation for university students is finding employment.	T	F
4	Yuriko does not think students really care much about reputation or facilities.	T	F
5	In the end, they agree together on one factor as the most important.	T	F
6	Yuriko believes that employers take the reputation of universities into account.	T	F

4 A TRIP TO REMEMBER

VOCABULARY

1 Complete the sentences with the words in the box.

> commuters   cockpit   departure lounge   diesel
> helmet   jet lag   motorists   motorway

1 The train was cancelled, which annoyed a lot of the .... who were waiting for it.

2 I've just come back from a trip to New York and now I'm suffering from ....

3 The plane was delayed on the runway so the pilots let us sit in the ....

4 Cars that run on .... are considered to be more harmful to the environment than those that run on petrol.

5 Although I've passed my driving test, I still get really nervous about driving on the ....

6 I think it should be compulsory for all cyclists to wear a .... when cycling on roads.

7 I was sitting in the .... when they announced that our flight had been cancelled.

8 They introduced a car sharing scheme in the city to reduce the number of .... on the roads.

2 Match words from column A and column B to make collocations.

Column A
1 prepare for
2 run on
3 overtake
4 leave
5 hold
6 avoid
7 harm
8 taxi

Column B
A a gap
B landing
C the rush hour traffic
D the environment
E the handlebars
F diesel
G on the runway
H the car in front

3 Choose the correct word to complete the sentences.

1 We booked our hotel at the *last / long* minute so we got a really good deal.

2 The room wasn't *air- / part*-conditioned so we had difficulty sleeping at night due to the heat.

3 I work *cut / part* time as a shop assistant during the school holidays.

4 They asked us to *apply / submit* our ideas online.

5 Despite the jetlag, I quite enjoy *far- / long*-distance air travel.

6 The company really liked the proposal so they *awarded / invested* money in it.

7 The company went bankrupt so they were offering *cut- / last*-price deals on all their package holidays.

8 The visitor *attraction / recreation* proved to be a big success with tourists.

9 The road was closed off to *members / representatives* of the public.

GRAMMAR

1 Read this extract from a tour guide. Write *a*, *an*, *the* or – (no article) in each gap.

(1) _____ Maldives is one of (2) _____ most unique countries in the world. It is made up of 1,192 islands, spread over 90,000 square kilometres. The capital, Malé, is unusual in that it is not (3) _____ tourist destination. It is less than six square miles, yet it is home to over (4) _____ third of the country's population of about 430,000. Only 185 of the islands are inhabited by local people. The others are dedicated to (5) _____ agriculture and tourism. Tourism accounts for (6) _____ most of the country's economy. The sun-drenched islands and coral reefs teeming with tropical fish attract tourists all year round. Sitting near (7) _____ equator, the islands enjoy temperatures between 26 and 30 degrees centigrade throughout the year. The Maldives is particularly popular with couples looking for (8) _____ amazing place to get married. The sun, sand and sea make these islands a paradise on (9) _____ earth. The Maldives is not (10) _____ budget destination, however. It has some of the most expensive and luxurious hotels in the world.

For each pair of sentences, choose one word from the 'Both' column to complete both gaps. You may need to make the word plural.

1 They say that cats have nine _____ .
_____ is what you make it.

2 Did you remember to bring your sports _____ ?
How many _____ does your bike have?

3 I haven't got _____ to finish my homework.
I've been to Italy three _____ .

4 Small _____ are finding it hard to survive.
Sam studied _____ at university.

5 Do you think there'll be _____ there for all my books?
We lived in a small flat when I was young – there were only three _____ .

6 They say this is a _____ of opportunity!
Farmers grow crops and raise animals on their _____ .

7 Doing my homework when it's sunny outside is a real _____ !
He was in a lot of _____ after he broke his leg skiing.

2 Put each noun into the correct column in the table.

| ~~things~~ ~~rice~~ ~~pain~~ data cash virus life crash business room pedal |
| footprint stuff resort scenery voyage land time chaos gear |

COUNTABLE	UNCOUNTABLE	BOTH
things	rice	pain

LISTENING PART 1

 09 **You will hear people talking in eight different situations. For questions 1–8, choose the best answer (A, B or C).**

1 You hear a man talking about a journey. How did he travel?
- **A** by bus
- **B** by plane
- **C** by train

2 You hear two people talking about the local bus service. What do they say about it?
- **A** The fares are too expensive.
- **B** The seats are uncomfortable.
- **C** The drivers are rude.

3 You hear two people talking about a place they have just visited. What kind of place is it?
- **A** an art gallery
- **B** a cinema
- **C** a shop

4 You hear a travel agent talking to a man about a holiday. What does she advise him to do?
- **A** purchase travel insurance
- **B** book excursions in advance
- **C** take warm clothing

5 You hear a man talking to a friend about a travel programme he has recently watched. What does he say about the programme?
- **A** It gave lots of useful advice.
- **B** It was better than he had expected.
- **C** It made him decide to visit a place.

6 You hear a woman talking about somewhere she has visited. What point is she making?
- **A** It appeals more to children than adults.
- **B** It reminded her of her childhood.
- **C** It is similar to another place she has visited.

7 You hear a man phoning a hotel. What does he want to find out?
- **A** how good the local transport services are
- **B** whether the hotel is suitable for children
- **C** when the restaurant opens in the evening

8 You hear a woman talking about a cruise she went on. What didn't she like about it?
- **A** the lack of variety
- **B** the food on board
- **C** the places they visited

SPEAKING PART 1

1 **10 Listen to four speakers answer a question in Part 1 of the Speaking test. Match the speakers to the questions they answer.**

A What do you do in the school holidays? ....

B Can you tell me about the place you come from? ....

C What type of holiday would you like to go on? ....

D How do you usually get to school? ....

2 **10 Listen again to the speakers. Complete the sentences with the words they use.**

Speaker 1

1 It's a .... little place, with just one shop, a school and not much else really.

2 There's no water close by, no lakes or rivers, so many people have swimming pools in their gardens because it's absolutely .... in summer.

Speaker 2

3 I haven't passed my driving test yet so I usually take the bus or .... to school.

4 In summer I might walk if I've got the .... , but that's not very often!

Speaker 3

5 It depends on the ....

6 During the winter holidays, we just .... out at each other's houses or go out for pizza or something like that.

Speaker 4

7 I'd probably .... a city break as I live in the countryside and big cities are much more exciting.

8 I'd definitely want to stay right in the centre, where all the .... is.

3 **This advice was given to a B2 First candidate before the Speaking test. Tick the good advice.**

1 Don't speak too quickly or too slowly. Slow down for important points and speed up a bit for less important details.

2 Stay up all night watching English films the night before the test.

3 Part 1 is just a practice so don't bother giving full answers.

4 You must speak only to the other candidate in Part 1.

5 Try to use a variety of vocabulary and grammar.

6 In Part 1 you might be asked Yes/No questions. You will still need to explain your answers and give examples and explanations.

7 Don't take your water into the exam.

5 GRAB SOME CULTURE

GRAMMAR

1 Complete the sentences with the correct form of the past simple, past perfect simple or past perfect continuous.

1 When we started using central heating, people in some Asian countries _____ (already / use) it for a few hundred years.

2 I _____ (begin) learning English at school in 2014, but I'd already learned many words by listening to songs in the language.

3 They suddenly realised that they _____ (forgot) to do their homework.

4 Mia _____ (only / play) the violin for two years when she was invited to join her local orchestra.

5 The teacher asked me whether I _____ (complete) the exercise.

6 When I _____ (see) the film at the cinema, it had been available online for a few weeks.

7 I _____ (think) about quitting my job before my friend told me that it wasn't a good idea.

8 They _____ (already / eat) their dinner by the time their father got home.

2 Find and correct the mistakes in the sentences below. Three sentences are correct.

1 I had been tired last night because I had been studying in the library the whole day.

2 I hadn't thought about studying languages at university until my teacher told me I should.

3 We already ate a big steak so I didn't really fancy eating desert.

4 We had been look for our cat, Joe, for three hours before we found him asleep under the bed.

5 I had just finished my assignment when I realised that I written about the wrong topic.

6 We were disappointed to hear that the show had been cancelled.

7 She asked if she could borrow my tablet but I had already lend it to someone else.

8 The film was actually much better than I had expected.

VOCABULARY

1 Choose three phrases for each description.

> bedtime reading   a real page-turner   tedious
> have me in stitches   I couldn't put it down
> she got me hooked   best-selling author
> confusing   heavy-going

1 I haven't been out all weekend because I downloaded *Yellow Crocus* by Laila Ibrahim. I wasn't able to do anything else until I'd finished it. She's written other novels but I absolutely loved this book – I'll definitely read anything else she publishes.

2 I know they are for children but I still find Roald Dahl's books really clever and they always make me laugh uncontrollably. More than 250 million copies of his books have been sold. I still have all my old copies and I sometimes pick one up and read for a bit before I sleep. They help me relax.

3 We had to read it for school but I didn't enjoy it at all. There was too much detailed description of every little thing. Our teacher explained how much skill the writer had used and how much care had gone into every detail of the structure, but I couldn't really get what the author was trying to say half the time.

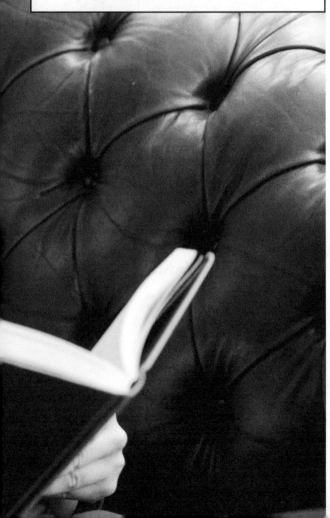

2 Complete the gaps in the conversation between Charlie and Nina. Use the words in the box.

> awful   deals with   dull
> gripping   set in   vital

Nina: Have you been watching that new drama series? The one **(1)** _____ Sweden.

Charlie: You mean the one where that family gets lost in the mountains? I watched one episode but I thought it was **(2)** _____, to be honest. It was so unbelievable and no one in it could act.

Nina: You're kidding! It **(3)** _____ some really important issues.

Charlie: Important issues? Such as what?

Nina: Well, if you had seen the second episode, you would have learnt a lot about how climate change has affected the environment in northern Europe.

Charlie: How very **(4)** _____ ! When you said important issues, I thought you meant social issues, not something boring like that.

Nina: How can you say that? Looking after the environment is **(5)** _____ . Despite what you say, I think it's great. It's really **(6)** _____ . I haven't missed a single episode.

PUSH YOURSELF C1

Choose a word or phrase from the box with a similar meaning to the underlined word or phrase in each sentence.

> absorbing   a must-read   contemporary   dense
> minor role   outstanding   remake   twists

1 I found the book *Never Let Me Go* really <u>gripping</u>. I just couldn't put it down.

2 Leonardo Di Caprio is an <u>exceptional</u> actor. He plays every role brilliantly.

3 I found the story quite difficult to follow. There were too many <u>complications</u> for my liking.

4 Dickens tells some marvellous stories but some of his books are very <u>heavy-going</u>.

5 In my view, that book is <u>compulsory reading</u> for everyone.

6 I had a <u>small part</u> in my school play.

7 I prefer <u>modern</u> literature to the classics.

8 Did you know there is another <u>new version</u> of *The Birds*?

For questions 1–8, read the text below and decide which answer (A, B, C or D) best fits each gap. There is an example at the beginning (0).

0 **A** section **B** piece **C** part **D** element

Art installations

An installation is more an experience than a **(0)** .... of art. **(1)** .... a painting or sculpture is created in the artist's studio and transported to a gallery, an installation is designed to fit a particular space. Many installations take up an entire room in a gallery, but they could also be **(2)** .... in the open. Installations put the viewer at the centre of the artwork. You may be able to walk through the space and the artist may **(3)** .... to different senses. There may be **(4)** .... of performance art, such as dance or mime, and nowadays computer technology may play a part. Recycled materials are often used, as **(5)** .... natural elements. Many installations are designed to **(6)** .... a concept rather than simply to be beautiful. Many **(7)** .... of this kind have been produced to support charities. Modern spectators engage with installations because they are now used to **(8)** .... in these kinds of experiences.

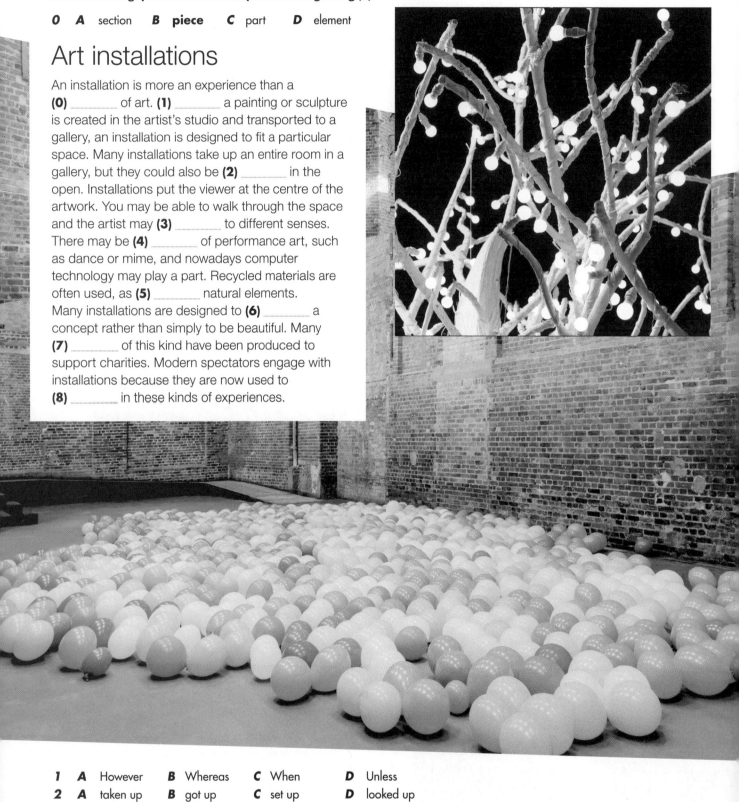

1	**A**	However	**B**	Whereas	**C**	When	**D**	Unless
2	**A**	taken up	**B**	got up	**C**	set up	**D**	looked up
3	**A**	appeal	**B**	use	**C**	design	**D**	attract
4	**A**	views	**B**	issues	**C**	roles	**D**	aspects
5	**A**	is	**B**	are	**C**	do	**D**	have
6	**A**	speak	**B**	commit	**C**	communicate	**D**	persuade
7	**A**	works	**B**	arts	**C**	performances	**D**	actions
8	**A**	enjoying	**B**	viewing	**C**	involving	**D**	participating

WRITING PART 2: ARTICLE

1 Read the Writing Part 2 task and an answer to the question written by a student called Alfie. Has he answered all the questions?

You see this notice on an English-language website.

Articles wanted!

Your favourite art form

What is your favourite art form? How did you become interested in it? What do you like about it? Who would you recommend it to?

We will publish the best articles on our website!

Write your article.

One of my favorite art forms is ballet. I first got into it when I was about eight years old and my parents took me to watch a performance at the local theatre. It was outstanding! From then on, I was hooked. I begged my mum to let me go to ballet classes after school and I was thriled when she did.

Ballet is elegant and graceful. The dancers seem quite fragile, but don't be fooled. Ballerinas are top-class atletes who train for many years to become the best at what they do. One of the reesons I love ballet so much is how effortless the dancers make it look.

If you're a fan of a good story and classicle music, then ballet is for you. That being said, I would incourage everyone to go and see a ballet show at some point in their lives.

---

2 Find <u>seven</u> spelling mistakes in the article.

3 Find the words and phrases in the article which mean the following.

1 became interested (paragraph 1)
2 really good (paragraph 1)
3 addicted (paragraph 1)
4 stylish (paragraph 2)
5 beautiful (paragraph 2)
6 easily done (paragraph 2)
7 someone who admires or supports something (paragraph 3)
8 at some moment in time (paragraph 3)

4 Where would you add the following sentences in the article? The first sentence has been done for you.

		WHICH PARAGRAPH?	AFTER WHICH SENTENCE IN THE PARAGRAPH?
0	Here, I learned a lot about the basics of ballet.	1	5
1	They also follow a strict diet to stay in the best possible shape.		
2	This is even more impressive when you consider that it's one of the most physically demanding art forms in the world.		
3	Trust me, you won't be disappointed!		

6 CLOSER TO NATURE

GRAMMAR

1 Match the two halves of the sentences.

1 There are millions of species
2 That beautiful park over there is the place
3 Tigers are on the 'red list'
4 Rainforests are forests
5 My friend Rebecca is an equine vet
6 I'd like you to meet Mr Jennings
7 That's the lion cub
8 He's the dog trainer

A who is the gardener here.
B which are characterised by high rainfall.
C who my mother takes our dog to.
D which means they are endangered.
E which means she treats sick horses.
F where we should have the picnic.
G which still haven't been discovered.
H which the rangers released into the wild.

2 Read the sentences you made in Exercise 1.

1 In which of the sentences is a comma needed between the two halves?
2 Why is a comma needed here?
3 Why is no comma needed in the other sentences?
4 In which sentences can the relative pronoun be omitted?
5 In which sentences can 'who' or 'which' be replaced by 'that'?

3 Complete the sentence with the correct relative pronoun.

1 I have never been back to the place .... I was born.
2 The safari park, ... was one of the first in the country, has closed down.
3 I would love to have a job .... involved working with animals.
4 That's the scientist .... I was telling you about last week.
5 Tasmania is an island .... is near Australia.
6 The building .... they made the scientific discovery is being demolished.

28

4 Add one of the phrases from the box to each sentence.

> on which   for which   along which
> both of whom   all of which   neither of which
> one of which   to whom

1 There are four species of zebra, ... are declining in number.
2 I grew up in the countryside, ... I am very grateful.
3 We have three cats, ... is a Siamese.
4 I have two sisters, ... like gardening.
5 Julie has a guide dog, ... she is totally dependent.
6 The man .... she wrote is an expert on plants.
7 We have two pear trees in our garden, ... bears fruit.
8 That's the path .... the elephants walk to get to the river.

5 Complete the gaps in the sentences with a preposition.

1 We need to prevent the black rhino .... dying out.
2 I don't approve .... testing cosmetic products on animals.
3 The farmer warned us .... entering the field with the bull.
4 The city is regarded .... one of the most beautiful places to live in the world.
5 Bees are capable .... producing only small amounts of honey.
6 My father insists .... cutting the grass every weekend.
7 They congratulated the guide .... a fantastic tour of the city.
8 I enquired .... getting a membership card for the zoo.

PUSH YOURSELF C1

In each sentence, either ONE or BOTH of the complex prepositions are correct. Put a line through those that are incorrect.

1 Photographers stayed up all night *in the hope of / by means of* getting pictures of the new-born lion cubs.
2 I love all animals *apart from / except for* snakes.
3 The pregnant panda is being moved to a new enclosure *ahead of / in front of* the birth.
4 I am writing *with regard to / in relation to* my recent visit to your wildlife park.
5 We made our decision *on the basis of / on account of* your previous experience with animals.
6 Richard went on the school trip to the zoo *on account of / along with* all the other students in his class.

VOCABULARY

1 Match each list to the correct phrase.

1 tiger, polar bear, mountain gorilla, bluefin tuna
2 forest, desert, grassland, wetlands
3 the Himalayas, the Alps, the Andes
4 climate change, water pollution, overfishing
5 solar, wind, hydropower, bioenergy
6 travelling by plane, using a computer, using plastic bags

A environmental issues
B renewable energy
C carbon footprint
D endangered species
E mountain ranges
F natural habitats

2 Choose the correct word to complete the sentences below.

1 We've just come back from a wonderful *travel / trip* to the Caribbean.
2 Please *say / tell* me what you think about the video I've just posted.
3 The closure of the zoo will have a negative *affect / effect* on the local economy.
4 The locals gave us some really good *advice / advise* on the best places to visit.
5 My sister is really *sensible / sensitive* and always cries when she watches wildlife documentaries.
6 I persuaded my cousin to let me *borrow / lend* her camera for my trip.
7 A lot of people often *chose / choose* to stay in hostels because they're cheaper than hotels.
8 We were not allowed to bring our own food onto the *sight / site*.

3 Complete the blog post with the words in the box.

> border   capital   famous   habitat
> heading   memorable   range
> unforgettable   vehicles   wildlife

Last month, my family and I went on a safari holiday to Africa. It was such an **(1)** _____ experience. We flew into Nairobi, which is the **(2)** _____ of Kenya, and then took a bus to Lake Nakuru. I had seen flamingos in the zoo close to where I live, but it was so much better seeing them in their natural **(3)** _____ . There were hundreds of them! We spent a few days there before **(4)** _____ south, through Nairobi, to Amboseli National Park. It's a stunning place, located on the Kenya–Tanzania **(5)** _____ . It's also close to Mount Kilimanjaro, which is the highest peak in the world that is not part of a mountain **(6)** _____ , standing at a height of 5,895 metres above sea level. The park is **(7)** _____ for being one to the best places in the world to see elephants and we spent five days there, travelling through the park. We weren't allowed to leave our **(8)** _____ at any point, which was understandable as there are very strict rules in place to protect the **(9)** _____ there. Sadly, after ten **(10)** _____ days in Kenya, we had to fly back home. I hope I can go back there again one day as it's one of the most beautiful places in the world.

 11 You will hear five people talking about their experience of being a volunteer. For questions 1–5, choose from the list (A–H) how each speaker feels about their experience. Use the letters only once. There are three extra letters which you do not need to use.

A proud of what they achieved
B embarrassed by a mistake they made
C annoyed by a person they worked with
D irritated by the lack of organisation
E impressed with the training they received
F bored by having to do the same thing many times
G relieved that they managed to complete the programme
H inspired by the feedback they received

Speaker 1 _____
Speaker 2 _____
Speaker 3 _____
Speaker 4 _____
Speaker 5 _____

WRITING PART 2: REVIEW

1 A student called Monty has written a review of a TV programme he watched. Complete the review with the adjectives in the box.

challenging   deadly   hilarious   entertaining   shaky   serious

Recently, I watched a documentary called Urban Monkeys. It was about monkeys who live in the cities of India. It was extremely **(1)** _____ as the animals tried every trick they could think of to get hold of food. The best bit was when a whole load of monkeys got into a school and somehow managed to open the children's lunch boxes and eat everything. It was **(2)** _____ . Although the programme was very amusing, there was a **(3)** _____ side to it as well. These creatures are a nuisance in Indian cities and can damage people's livelihoods. In addition, they carry **(4)** _____ diseases so they pose a real threat to the inhabitants of these cities. It must have been **(5)** _____ to film this documentary because the monkeys move around very quickly and they can climb onto buildings. At times, the camerawork was a bit **(6)** _____ , but you can't really blame the film-makers for that.
Overall, it was a fascinating programme for all the family.

2 Which words or phrases does Monty use to do these things?

1 Say when he watched this programme?
2 Introduce his favourite part?
3 Introduce an opposite idea?
4 Introduce a similar point?
5 Introduce his conclusion?

3 Match the words (1–4) with the phrases (A–D) to create collocations.

1 damage   **A** someone for something
2 carry   **B** a threat to someone or something
3 pose   **C** someone's livelihood
4 blame   **D** diseases

4 Find three different ways in which Monty refers to the monkeys.

7 WHAT'S IN YOUR FOOD?

GRAMMAR

1 Read the texts and answer the questions.

"I wish my sister would clear up the kitchen after she cooks. She spills food all over the place and I have to clear it up before Mum comes home. The food she cooks always smells great, though. I usually try to get some leftovers but there never are any. Her friends are so greedy!"

Nisha (female, 18)

"If only I'd learned to cook when I had the chance! I'm at university now and I have to eat takeaways and convenience foods, which I don't really enjoy. It's also very expensive. My parents told me I should learn, but I was too busy with my exams. I should have listened to them."

Yohan (male, 20)

"My favourite food is Japanese. It looks so elegant and it's also really healthy. The trouble is it's so expensive here. If only I lived in Japan! I wish Japanese food was cheaper – and it would be great if they gave you a bit more in the restaurants!"

Olivia (female, 22)

"I've been studying catering at college for the last few months. I really hope to have a restaurant of my own one day. I want to serve fusion food – that means food which mixes different cuisines, so things like Polish curry – things that have never been done before. I love cooking! I just wish I'd started the course when I was younger."

Tomasz (male, mid-30s)

1 Who regrets not following good advice?
2 Who would like their favourite food to be cheaper?
3 Who gets annoyed with someone else's behaviour?
4 Who has food-related ambitions?
5 Who wants someone to share with them?
6 Who regrets waiting so long to do something?

2 Read the texts again. Complete each gap with up to FOUR words, using the correct form of the word in brackets.

1 Olivia .... in Japan. (*wish*)
2 Yohan .... to cook when he was living at home. (*wish*)
3 Nisha .... with her sister. (*annoy*)
4 Tomasz .... starting the course earlier. (*regret*)
5 Yohan .... have to live on takeaways and convenience food. (*wish*)
6 Nisha wishes her sister's friends .... so greedy. (*be*)
7 Olivia .... the portion sizes in Japanese restaurants were bigger. (*wish*)

3 Find and correct the mistakes in the sentences below. Three sentences are correct. Decide if the sentences are third or mixed conditionals.

1 That menu looked amazing. If I'd been there, I would choose the goat's cheese and pear salad.
2 If my grandmother had eaten the way we do now, she wouldn't have lived to be 100.
3 If I didn't forget to put the lasagne in the fridge last night, we could have eaten it now.
4 I'd spent less money if I had gone to the market instead of the supermarket.
5 The cake would be tastier if you'd remembered to add sugar.
6 If we hadn't eaten so much junk food when we were young, we would be healthier now.
7 If my uncle would have gone to catering college, he would be a professional chef.

Choose the correct adverb for each sentence.

1 *Apparently / Ultimately*, they've found out that butter is good for you, even though they've been telling us not to eat it for years.
2 *Undoubtedly / Remarkably*, milk costs less now than it did five years ago.
3 *Ultimately / Supposedly*, you have to follow the diet that suits your lifestyle and budget.
4 *Supposedly / Inevitably*, you lose weight if you eat very little on two days of the week.
5 *Apparently / Inevitably*, I gave up my diet after a week.
6 *Undoubtedly / Remarkably*, eating five portions of fresh fruit and vegetables every day is a good idea.

VOCABULARY

1 Complete each gap with a word or phrase from the box. There are two words you do not need to use.

stick to	gone off	savoury	supplements	allergic
in season	portions	decor	appetite	ambiance

1 **A:** Is there anything you don't eat?
  B: Yes, shellfish. I'm _____ to it.
2 Do you prefer sweet or _____ food?
3 **A:** Why are these strawberries so expensive?
  B: Because they're not _____ at the moment.
4 I really love the _____ of that restaurant. The candlelight and soft music are so romantic.
5 **A:** You haven't eaten very much.
  B: No, I've lost my _____ . I think I might be ill.
6 I tried to be a vegetarian but I couldn't _____ it for very long.
7 That meat smells terrible. I think it's _____ .
8 What I love most about that restaurant is that the _____ are so big. One meal is enough for both of us.

2 Match the word groups (1–7) to the prefixes (A–G).

1 appear, approve, obey, like
2 fair, necessary, helpful, aware
3 legal, logical, legible, legitimate
4 responsible, rational, regular, relevant
5 behave, lead, understand, place
6 discover, write, apply, unite
7 patient, mature, practical, possible

A dis-
B il-
C im-
D ir-
E mis-
F re-
G un-

3 Complete the sentences with one of the new words in Exercise 2 in the correct form.

1 A new law in the UK has made it .... for teenagers under the age of sixteen to buy energy drinks.
2 I think he .... me because he did the exact opposite of what I told him to do.
3 I had to .... the whole essay as my tutor told me it was all factually incorrect.
4 I was .... of the fact that lemons contain more sugar than strawberries until my teacher told me about it this morning.
5 I love eating broccoli but my brother really .... it. It make him feel sick!
6 I think it's .... of people to throw away plastic bottles. They should try to reuse them as much as possible.

READING AND USE OF ENGLISH PART 2

For questions 1–8, read the text below and think of the word which best fits each gap. Use only one word in each gap. There is an example at the beginning (0).

We all know **(0)** ___how___ successful advertising is. The adverts we remember most are probably for everyday things **(1)** .... as soft drinks, sweets and convenience foods. We all know what we should **(2)** .... eating – healthy food, such as fruit and vegetables. The trouble is, these foods are never advertised!

So, what would happen **(3)** .... advertisers used all their sophisticated techniques to try to sell healthy food to children? Maybe they could make vegetables seem cool and fruit the thing teenagers want to be seen eating. Most of **(4)** .... would agree that it would be a good thing, but the trouble is farmers and fruit growers do not have enough money to spend **(5)** .... advertising.

So, who would pay **(6)** .... it? Governments, for a start, as they would save money if people **(7)** .... healthier. Local businesses could contribute and celebrities could be asked to give their time for free. After **(8)** .... , everybody wants a healthier future generation.

SPEAKING PARTS 3 AND 4

1 🎧 12 Listen to Sofia and Enrique deciding which type of food to have for an end of term party. What do they decide to eat?

2 Why don't they choose these other options? Match each option (1–4) to a reason (A–D) they don't choose it.

1 tea, coffee and cake
2 everyone cooks a dish and brings it
3 snack foods such as crisps, nuts and popcorn
4 a formal dinner at a restaurant

A It's not very healthy.
B It's too expensive.
C It's not special enough.
D It's too difficult.

3 Match what Sofia and Enrique say (1–7) with a function (A–G).

1 What do you think?
2 You've got a point.
3 So what about going for a pizza?
4 It's cheap and pretty convenient.
5 Definitely not!
6 Oh, come on! There must be something simple you could make.
7 It might turn out better than you think.

A giving an opinion
B making a suggestion
C speculating
D trying to persuade
E agreeing
F asking for an opinion
G disagreeing

4 🎧 13 Listen to four speakers answer different questions (A–D). Match each speaker to the question they were asked.

Speaker 1 ....
Speaker 2 ....
Speaker 3 ....
Speaker 4 ....

A Can you tell me about a special meal you've had recently?
B What kind of restaurants are popular with people in your country?
C What foods do you eat on festival days in your country?
D Do people in your country usually eat a meal with their family every day?

5 🎧 13 Listen to the speakers again. Complete the sentences with the missing words.

1 It takes quite a long time to make, which is why it's really ....
2 My grandma is an amazing cook and my aunts and uncles usually bring cakes and .... , so I always enjoy Sunday lunch.
3 The food is really tasty and .... and you can ask them to make it less spicy if you want.
4 I ate so much that I was absolutely .... !

8 LIVING MADE EASY

GRAMMAR

1 Do these pairs of sentences have similar or different meanings? Write S (same) or D (different) for each one.

1   **A**   Connor can't have been driving the car at the time of the accident.
    B   There is a chance that Connor was driving the car at the time of the accident.

2   **A**   My computer suddenly stopped working yesterday – I think it might have crashed.
    B   It is possible that my computer has crashed.

3   **A**   The virus may have come from that email you opened.
    B   The virus definitely came from that email you opened.

4   **A**   There may be life on other planets.
    B   Some people believe there is life on other planets.

5   **A**   The plants have all died – she must have forgotten to water them.
    B   I believe she didn't water her plants, which is why they died.

6   **A**   Black holes might lead to other parts of the universe.
    B   It is a fact that black holes lead to other parts of the universe.

7   **A**   There must be other sources of renewable energy.
    B   There will be problems if we don't find other sources of renewable energy.

2 Complete each gap with two or three words, including a modal verb of deduction or speculation. There may be more than one correct answer.

1   Peter .... stuck in traffic. He's never normally late.

2   Michael lost his job last month. It .... easy for him since then.

3   I wonder why my computer isn't working properly. It .... due to the recent upgrade or perhaps there's a problem with the battery.

4   I'm not sure why I got such a low mark for my biology essay. I think I .... misread the question, or perhaps my grammar let me down.

5   That's my sister on the phone again. She .... forgotten to tell me something the first time she rang.

6   There .... life on Mars. The aliens would have visited us by now!

3 Match the two halves of the sentences.

1   My mother used to sing that song
2   Can you pass me
3   I can't believe they offered
4   You should write a letter
5   I lent my brother
6   My auntie bought me
7   Arjun gave his uncle

A   the electrician's phone number.
B   to me when I was a child.
C   of complaint to the manager.
D   a new jumper for my birthday.
E   that test tube, please?
F   my car for a few days.
G   me the job!

4 Tick the correct sentences. Correct those which contain an error.

1 You need to tell to me the truth.
2 Can you pour for me another cup of tea, please?
3 I taught them a new card game.
4 Can you do for me a favour?
5 I used to send my friend a postcard when I went on holiday.
6 The teacher read the instructions out to the class.
7 Leila gave to her cousin some good advice.

PUSH YOURSELF C1

Complete the sentences with the words in the box. Add capital letters to the words if necessary.

appears	likelihood	possibly
realistically	suggests	though

1 In all _____ , the computer developed a virus, which is why it's not working.
2 It looks as _____ the servers might have overheated.
3 Scientific evidence _____ that mobile phones can cause health problems later in life.
4 My laptop can't _____ have developed an issue. I bought it only last week!
5 It _____ that the funding has been withdrawn so we'll probably need to pull the plug on the project.
6 _____ speaking, we don't have a chance of meeting the deadline next Monday.

VOCABULARY

1 Complete the second sentence so that it has a similar meaning to the first sentence, using the word given. Do not change the word given. Use between two and four words.

1 We misunderstood each other.
   GOT
   We _____ crossed.
2 Milton has lost his enthusiasm for the project.
   OUT
   Milton has _____ steam.
3 This is very easy to understand.
   NOT
   It is _____ science.
4 Jake loses his temper easily.
   SHORT
   Jake _____ fuse.
5 Amy suddenly understood the English grammar point the teacher was making.
   BULB
   Amy _____ moment and understood the English grammar point the teacher was making.
6 The company decided to withdraw support for the project.
   PULL
   The company decided _____ on the project.

2 🔊 14 Listen to the speakers. Which of the words in the box are they talking about? There are two words that you don't need to use.

breakthroughs	backup	network	spreadsheets
screenshot	upgrades	icons	browse

Speaker 1 _____   Speaker 4 _____
Speaker 2 _____   Speaker 5 _____
Speaker 3 _____   Speaker 6 _____

LISTENING PART 2

🔊 15 **You will hear a marine biologist called Marie Jackson talking about her work with seahorses. For questions 1–10, complete the sentences with a word or short phrase.**

1   A seahorse pregnancy lasts for _____ weeks.

2   Most new-born seahorses do not _____ .

3   When seahorse couples see each other in the morning, they do a dance and _____ .

4   Marie compares the way seahorses eat to an _____ .

5   Because they need lots of food, seahorses have excellent _____ .

6   Marie describes seahorses as _____ animals because they are very sensitive to injury.

7   It is particularly important for people interested in seahorses to avoid using a camera _____ .

8   Some people consume seahorses as they believe it will make them
    _____ .

9   Marie supports _____ on taking seahorses out of the oceans and selling them.

10 Those who want to help could make a note of their sightings of seahorses or even _____ a seahorse.

WRITING PART 2: REPORT

1 Read the Writing Part 2 task and the sample report. Complete the gaps with words from the box. Add capital letters to the words if necessary.

A website on learning English is collecting reports from different countries on how technology is used in schools around the world.

Write a report on the use of technology to learn English in your country. You should:

- summarise the current situation
- recommend how the use of technology could be improved.

| the problem is | however | findings | opinions |
| recommendations | introduction | the most useful thing |

Using technology to learn English in South Korea

(1) ....

I asked students of English in Seoul what kind of technology they use to learn English and which they think is the most useful. Altogether 17 students studying at language schools and high schools gave me their views.

(2) ....

The main finding was that every student I spoke to uses online resources and apps to practise their English. Most students shared the following **(3)** .... :

- There is plenty of online material and many suitable apps for learning English. **(4)** .... that there is not enough guidance on which are the best for different types of students and which should be avoided.
- Using apps is really useful for students in their self-study time. Most learners, **(5)** .... , prefer to work in groups and engage with their teacher during class time.
- **(6)** .... about technology is that it is now easy to gain access to English films, songs and texts. These are even more popular than materials designed specifically for language learning.

(7) ....

1. Teachers should limit technology use in class and interact with students instead.
2. Schools should recommend the best websites and apps for students.

2 Match the words from the report (1–7) to the definitions (A–G).

1	altogether	A	interact with people
2	views	B	learning on your own
3	guidance	C	for a particular reason
4	self-study	D	restrict
5	engage	E	advice or help
6	specifically	F	in total
7	limit	G	opinions

3 Rearrange the words below to form phrases that you can use in your report.

Introduction

1 the / of / this / describe / report / is / to / aim

....

2 report / this / inform / intended / is / to

....

3 purpose / is / of / to / the / this / main / report / provide

....

Advantages and disadvantages

4 main / one / is / the / this / of / of / advantages

....

5 aspects / of / the / this / positive / are

....

6 of / to / this / the / drawbacks / is / one

....

Recommendations

7 strongly / would / that / suggest / I

....

8 ideal / this / would / be / for

....

9 to / want / consider / might / we

....

9 THE GREAT OUTDOORS

GRAMMAR

1 Choose the correct future form for each sentence. In some sentences, both forms are possible.

1 In another decade, we'll all *be wearing / wear* 'smart suits', or wearable computers.

2 By the middle of the century, people *will become / will be becoming* younger instead of older.

3 It is more than likely that the buildings of the future *might be / will be* able to talk to us.

4 Some scientists believe that by 2040 we *will have given up / will be giving up* using computers.

5 In all probability, the weather *will eventually be / will have eventually been* controlled by humans.

6 Within a few years, scientists *will have developed / will be developing* meat grown in laboratories.

7 In 250 million years, all the continents *will join up / will have joined up* into one large block of land.

8 In a few hundred years, we may no longer *be speaking / have spoken* English.

2 Complete each sentence with the correct form of the future perfect or the future continuous, using the words in the brackets.

1 In April, I _____ (work) in the new conference centre that's being built.

2 What do you think you _____ (achieve) in five years' time?

3 We _____ (watch) the big game after 8 pm.

4 By July next year, I _____ (finish) my course at college.

5 Where did they say they _____ (go) tomorrow?

6 This time next week, we _____ (swim) in the sea.

7 I _____ (already / prepare) the dinner by the time you get home tonight.

8 I think we _____ (communicate) via hologram at some point in the future.

3 Correct the errors in these sentences. There may be more than one way to correct each error. Tick the three sentences that are correct.

1 Scientists are trying to figure out what kind of fuel could be used to get astronauts to Mars and back.

2 There is prospect of finding life on Mars during my lifetime.

3 It is possible that researchers will be finding a cure for the common cold in the near future.

4 Do you think people will be eating lab-grown meat at some point in the future?

5 In 200 years' time, some inhabited islands are disappearing under the sea.

6 Will chimpanzees be becoming extinct by the end of the century?

7 I really believe that humans will be living on another planet in the year 3000.

8 There's a chance that robots will be replaced most manual workers by 2050.

PUSH YOURSELF C1

Complete the sentences with the phrases in the box.

counting down the days	get around to
just around the corner	sign of things to come
sooner or later	

1 I'll _____ washing the car this afternoon.

2 We'll find a solution to the problem _____ .

3 There are university courses that can be done completely online. It's a _____ .

4 I believe the day that people start using driverless cars is _____ .

5 I'm _____ until we go on holiday.

VOCABULARY

1 Complete the words to form sentences.

1 The sea is very rough because of the g _____
   _____ – f _____ winds.

2 D _____ _____ fog means that driving
   conditions will be extremely poor.

3 The bridge has been closed due to the v _____
   _____ _____ storms.

4 The s _____ _____ temperatures
   have led to a water shortage in some areas.

5 The storms are set to continue with h _____ _____
   _____ rain predicted for most areas.

6 The clouds will move away leading to b _____
   _____ _____ skies in the afternoon.

2 Write the correct prepositions in the gaps.

1 The sun came _____ at around seven
   this morning.

2 The wind seems to be dying _____ .
   Perhaps we can go sailing today after all.

3 Oh no, it's starting to cloud _____ .
   I hope it won't rain.

4 The wind seems to be picking _____ again.
   Maybe I'll hang the clothes out to dry.

5 The pond in our village freezes _____ every
   winter. You can skate on it during the coldest
   months.

6 The hurricane ripped _____ the town,
   destroying everything in its path.

7 The weather seems to be brightening _____ .
   Let's go for a swim!

3 Choose the correct spelling of each word.

1 persistant / persistent
2 humidity / humiditie
3 visibility / vissibility
4 changable / changeable
5 gloryous / glorious
6 downpour / downpor
7 feirce / fierce

4 Make collocations using words from Exercise 3.

1 _____ sunshine
2 _____ rain
3 a heavy _____
4 a _____ storm
5 poor _____
6 stifling _____
7 _____ weather

5 Put the words in the correct columns in the table. For each one, use a suffix to form a new word with a similar meaning, making any other necessary changes.

| ~~celebrate~~ evident colour compete refer develop decide |
| meaning private hesitate biology achieve special accurate |

-ATION	-ENCE	-MENT	-IST	-FUL	-IVE	-ACY
celebration						

6 Complete the sentences below with a word from Exercise 5.

1 There is no scientific .... to suggest that life exists on other planets.
2 It was a wonderful birthday .... All of his friends and family were there.
3 She works as a .... and spends a lot of her time in the lab.
4 Sending humans to Mars would be an amazing ....
5 My brother is really .... He always wants to win.
6 Satellites are able to track down our location with amazing ....

READING AND USE OF ENGLISH PART 3

For questions 1–8, read the text below. Use the word given in capitals at the end of some of the lines to form a word that fits in the gap in the same line. There is an example at the beginning (0).

Life on board the International Space Station

Have you ever wondered what life is like on the International Space Station? In many ways, it is like life on Earth, but there are some major **(0)** _differences_ . **DIFFERENT**
For one thing, astronauts need to exercise for at least two hours a day to prevent bone and muscle loss. The **(1)** .... they use is different to what **EQUIP**
we use on Earth because in space people are weightless. Another thing is that food is **(2)** .... different because, rather unsurprisingly, there is not **SLIGHT**
much **(3)** .... space on board. Most food is dried and the astronauts are **STORE**
(4) .... to use things like salt and pepper as they will typically fly away! **ABLE**
Instead they use **(5)** .... designed liquid seasoning. **SPECIAL**
What **(6)** .... do astronauts do in their free time? They can watch films, **ACTIVE**
read or play games but most enjoy looking out of the window. The sunrise, which occurs every 45 minutes, can be **(7)** .... When they are **SPECTACLE**
sleeping, they have to make sure they are strapped in so that they cannot move. If they became **(8)** .... , they could fly around and hurt **TIE**
themselves.

SPEAKING PART 1

1 Are these statements about Part 1 of the Speaking test True or False?

1 In Part 1, the candidates discuss something together.
2 Each candidate will be asked at least four different questions.
3 The questions in Part 1 are related to familiar topics.
4 Part 1 lasts about two minutes.
5 Part 1 is designed to be the most difficult.

2 🔊 16 **Listen to two students' answers to a Part 1 question, 'Tell us about a place you have visited in your country'. Complete the table.**

	HONZA, CZECH REPUBLIC	ALICIA, SPAIN
Name of the place	*Kutná Hora*	*Ciudad Encantada*
Why people visit		
The atmosphere of the place		
Adjectives used to describe the place		
The speaker's opinion		

3 🔊 16 **Listen again. Complete the sentences with the words the speakers use. Then match the sentences to the grammatical structures (A–E) they use.**

1 **Honza:** ... such as the Cathedral of St Barbara, ... really stunning!

2 **Honza:** Actually, I would say it's just .... Prague.

3 **Honza:** If you ...., I'd definitely recommend a visit.

4 **Alicia:** The name means Enchanted City and it really is .... place I've ever seen.

5 **Alicia:** Over many years, the rocks .... into strange shapes.

A a passive structure
B a relative clause
C a conditional sentence
D a superlative
E a comparative

4 **Reorder the words to form correct sentences. Add punctuation if necessary.**

1 I / buildings / full / London / last / is / summer / historic / which / of / visited

2 as / just / be / countryside / can / winter / summer / in / as / beautiful / the / in

3 I'd / the / get / go / you / that / chance / suggest / there / you / if / definitely

4 would / is / beautiful / world / I / that / in / one / world / say / Istanbul / of / the / cities / the / most

5 the / over / extended / the / has / museum / 10 / last / been / years

10 TO THE LIMIT

GRAMMAR

1 Complete the second sentence so that it has a similar meaning to the first sentence, using the word given. Do not change the word given. You must use between two and five words.

1 My parents say I can't play video games on weekdays.
LET
My parents _____ play video games on weekdays.

2 I will call Taro to see whether he can give you swimming lessons.
ARRANGE
I will try to _____ give you swimming lessons.

3 Geeta needs the coach to repair her tennis racket.
GET
Geeta has to _____ by the coach.

4 We are forced to get up at 5 am for training by the coach.
MAKES
Our coach _____ at 5 am for training.

5 I need to finish writing my report before the meeting.
GET
I must _____ before the meeting.

6 A famous fashion designer is going to design our new kit.
HAVE
We are going to _____ by a famous fashion designer.

PUSH YOURSELF C1

Complete the second sentence using a cleft sentence so that it has a similar meaning to the first sentence. There is an example to help you (0).

0 I love hiking because of the views.
What I *love about hiking is the views.*

1 My brother got me interested in tennis.
It was _____ .

2 I enjoy bungee jumping because of the excitement.
The thing _____ .

3 I go running every day to keep fit.
The reason _____ .

4 I love playing sport because of the competition.
What I _____ .

5 Baseball is really popular in my country.
One activity _____ .

2 Read the article and choose the correct option for each pair of words.

The Goal for Life Foundation was set up in 2011 to **(1)** *help / let* children from disadvantaged backgrounds to reach their sporting goals. The charity arranges for professional footballers **(2)** *coach / to coach* the boys and girls for free – everyone involved is a volunteer. The regular training sessions **(3)** *cause / let* children develop their skills in an enjoyable and supportive environment. The charity has managed to **(4)** *have / get* local shops and restaurants to provide sports kits, equipment and meals for the students. It has been wonderful to see the community support for the Foundation. The organisers allow parents **(5)** *come / to come* along too to offer support and encouragement to their children. The Co-ordinator of Goal for Life, Chris Roberts, said: 'It's important to **(6)** *help / get* children interested in sports from an early age. As well as the health benefits, it **(7)** *helps / allows* them develop self-confidence. We have also seen some wonderful friendships develop here.'

3 Write the correct form of the adjective in brackets to complete the sentences.

1 I tried to learn how to code but I found it really _____ . (*confuse*)

2 I was _____ to hear that they had been eliminated from the competition. (*shock*)

3 I don't know about you, but I find the commentator really _____ . (*irritate*)

4 We went to the new restaurant and the musicians they had there were _____ . (*amaze*)

5 Personally, I found the film _____ but I know others absolutely loved it. (*disappoint*)

6 My friends and I were really _____ after our 10 km run. (*exhaust*)

7 The fact that I had been accepted onto the programme was _____ . (*excite*)

8 I know some of my friends couldn't stand the presenter, but I found him _____ . (*fascinate*)

VOCABULARY

1 For each gap, choose a word from the box and write it in the correct form.

compete	decide	excite
impress	spectate	separate

1 The _____ was made to cancel the match due to the poor weather.

2 The _____ gave the players a standing ovation as they walked onto the pitch.

3 The _____ begins next week and over 100 teams have entered.

4 The fans had to be _____ due to the fierce rivalry.

5 Everyone was singing and dancing. You could feel the _____ in the stadium.

6 The fact that she was unbeaten throughout the whole tournament was really _____ .

2 Read the definitions and then complete each word. The first two letters are given to help you.

1 A person who is very good at sports, particularly in a competitive way. at_____

2 A person or team who competes against you in a sports competition or debate. op_____

3 People who watch a sports event but do not necessarily support one team or competitor. sp_____

4 The fans of a particular team or competitor. su_____

5 People who are watching a concert, play, film or TV show. au_____

6 A person who takes part in a competition. co_____

3 17 Listen to two students, Jan and Isabel, answering the question 'Should the working week be reduced from five days to four?'

1 Who agrees and who disagrees?

2 Who makes the following points?

A Technological advances make our work easier.

B Computers and other devices take up more of our time.

C People nowadays have more spare time than people did in the past.

D Lots of people have jobs or follow courses away from the place they come from.

E People need only a little more free time.

F The problem of lack of time is worse for young people.

4 17 Listen again and complete the sentences with the words or phrases you hear.

Jan

1 I know that _____ the past we have a lot of leisure time.

2 _____ , life in general is a lot busier than it was.

3 _____ , we have to update our social media.

4 There's a lot of pressure on young people _____ .

Isabel

5 _____ , I feel that most of us have about the right amount of leisure time.

6 _____ , for most of us work is not as hard as it was in the past.

7 _____ , lots of people have to move far away from their hometown.

8 But _____ , we don't need a three-day weekend every week.

1 🔊 **18 You will hear five short extracts in which people are talking about an activity they do during their leisure time. For questions 1–5, choose from the list (A–H) one disadvantage of the activity that the speaker mentions. Use the letters only once. There are three extra letters which you do not need to use.**

Speaker 1 ....
Speaker 2 ....
Speaker 3 ....
Speaker 4 ....
Speaker 5 ....

A The activity can be expensive.
B There is a danger of getting hurt.
C A good fitness level is needed.
D It can be very time-consuming.
E People take competitions too seriously.
F You have to buy a lot of equipment.
G It's too mentally challenging.
H Men and women are treated differently.

2 **Check your answers to Exercise 1. Do these extracts help you find the answers or distract you from them? Write A (answer) or D (distractor) for each one.**

Speaker 1

1 It's true you need a lot of equipment, but most people hire it.

2 Even for recreational diving, you do have to be quite fit.

3 … diving as a hobby is not nearly as risky as people think.

Speaker 2

4 You also need to be a risk-taker because injury is always a possibility.

5 Some equipment is used only by men, some only by women and some by both.

Speaker 3

6 The cost of keeping him there is lower because the school uses him for lessons.

7 I feel that people get too competitive in this sport.

Speaker 4

8 You have to concentrate really hard and plan a lot of moves ahead.

1 **19 Read the task below. Then listen to Todd and Christina discuss the task. Which facility do they agree is the best idea?**

A bowling centre

A cinema complex

A swimming pool

Your town has decided to spend some money on ONE of these leisure facilities.

A library

A community park

2 **19 Listen again. How many of the options do they discuss?**

3 **19 Listen again. Underline the discourse markers you hear.**

besides	in that case
for example	such as
to be honest	anyway
in comparison to	I think
on balance	

4 **Read the two Part 4 questions and the replies given by a candidate called Mai. Then answer the questions.**

Question 1

Do you think governments should spend more money on sports and leisure facilities?

That's quite a difficult question because the government has so many things to spend money on. Some people might say that there are more important things than tennis courts and running tracks – for example, hospitals and schools. However, in my view, we shouldn't underestimate the value of all types of leisure, not just sports. I mean, people are more likely to get sick if they don't have enough relaxation and that could cost more money in the long run.

1 Does the candidate answer the question?
2 What is her opinion?
3 What discourse markers does she use?
4 Underline the sports and leisure-related vocabulary she uses.

Question 2

Do you think sports should be compulsory in schools?

Well, this might be an unpopular view, but no, I don't. For me, when you force people to do something, that thing becomes less attractive to them. The aim of schools should be to get young people to develop a lifelong love of sports and exercise. So what they need to do is let students choose whether to do sports or not, and then make it fun and not too competitive so that even those who are not naturally sporty want to take part.

1 Does the candidate answer the question?
2 What is her opinion?
3 What discourse markers does she use?
4 Underline the sports and leisure-related vocabulary she uses.

11 FACT OR FICTION?

GRAMMAR

1 Change each sentence into reported speech. Use *said* or *asked*.

Example
'People listened to the radio much more in my day,' said Harry.
Harry said that people listened / had listened to the radio much more in his day.

1 'We're going to see *Dream Girls* at the theatre next Thursday.'
Sophie _____

2 'What kind of news stories do you like to read?'
Alain _____

3 'Have you ever taken part in a play before?'
The teacher _____

4 'My sister can sing really well but I'm a hopeless singer.'
Carlos _____

5 '*The Shape of Water* was directed by Guillermo del Toro.'
The article _____

6 'If there's an action film showing, I'll come with you to the cinema.'
Leyla _____

2 Complete each gap with one of the reporting verbs.

suggested	threatened	criticised	denied
promised	explained	refused	

1 My parents always _____ me for spending too much time watching TV.

2 My dad _____ to turn off the internet connection if I didn't do my homework.

3 Patrick _____ to arrange some brilliant entertainment for my party.

4 Mr Wyatt _____ to help us rehearse for the talent show because he said it would give us an unfair advantage.

5 Andy _____ giving Wendy the best part because she was his cousin – he said it was because she was the best dancer.

6 Someone _____ having the party on a boat but I was against the idea.

7 Ben _____ why he didn't enjoy the show – he said the story was confusing.

3 Correct the mistakes in these sentences.

1 He said me he would meet me after the show.

2 Bethany asked me where did we get the costumes for the school play from.

3 The man who ran the theatre asked whether I can sing.

4 One of my friends suggested we going to the opera for a change.

5 Freddie told the DJ play a different song.

6 Emma asked whether had we read the article.

7 The waiter said that he will blow up the balloons.

VOCABULARY

1 Choose the most appropriate word to complete the sentences.

1 When they developed the concept of the show, their target *audience / influence* was teenagers, but they later found that a lot of adults watched it too.

2 They organised a big media campaign to *embrace / promote* the show, but the viewing figures were really low, so they pulled the plug on it.

3 The government is taking action against social media sites which, they argue, have too much *influence / reality* on what people think.

4 A lot of the articles they publish in their newspaper aren't *credible / reality* as they don't do any background research on the facts.

5 The number of people who read articles online instead of in newspapers is *needed / predicted* to grow in the future.

6 The number of *spectators / viewers* watching the show increased dramatically during the second series.

7 The radio show failed to *attract / welcome* a big enough audience, so they ended up cancelling it.

2 Match the words from column A with the words from column B to make collocations. Then match them to quotations 1–6.

Column A		Column B	
1	go	**A**	time
2	brand	**B**	viral
3	prime	**C**	censorship
4	reality	**D**	privacy
5	invasion of	**E**	awareness
6	media	**F**	shows

Complete the sentences with the words in the box. Add capital letters to the words if necessary.

all things   in light   it speaks   on the assumption regardless of

1 .... for itself that many TV companies charge more for advertising during prime-time hours.

2 .... considered, social media has given people more access to news from around the world.

3 .... of the new rules that ban junk food advertising on TV, the number of teenagers eating fast food has decreased.

4 .... the fact that it can damage your eyes, the number of hours people spend in front of a screen has increased dramatically.

5 The newspaper has started to invest more money in improving its website .... that more people will use it in the future.

> **1** In my country, the government controls what is shown on TV and printed in the newspapers.

> **2** That clip was shared so widely that I think everyone on social media saw it.

> **3** I love watching TV programmes about people's lives – they are so entertaining.

> **4** The best programmes are usually on at around 8 to 10 pm, when lots of people will be watching TV.

> **5** I think young people nowadays have a good knowledge of companies and what they make.

> **6** The biggest problem with being famous is that journalists never leave you in peace.

You are going to read an extract from a novel in which a girl called Raquel takes part in a play at her local drama club. For questions 1–6, choose the answer (A, B, C or D) which you think fits best according to the text.

I had truly believed I would get the part of Shirley. To say I was devastated that it was given to Jodie would have been an understatement. I had been convinced that I was in every way more suited to the part than she was. My long, dark hair and athletic build were much more similar to the character described in the novel than Jodie's classic blond good looks. And this was a musical – Shirley had to sing and that was another reason I should have got the part. To make matters worse, I'd just been asked to play one of Shirley's friends. Apart from the role of Shirley, the other main parts were for males, but that didn't bother me. I'd have happily put on a false beard, but no, all the other important parts had gone to the boys.

Rehearsals went on for eight weeks over the hottest part of the summer. At first, I'll confess, I wanted Jodie to fail, but as time went by I had to admit she wasn't bad. I think she must have taken some singing lessons since our previous production. She certainly had a better memory than I did. I struggled with my lines, whereas she always had hers perfectly memorised. It occurred to me that that might be why I hadn't got a bigger part. Even in the theatre, looks aren't everything, I realised.

That summer was more enjoyable than I'd expected it to be. Our director, Matthew, made the rehearsals fun, bringing us ice cream and telling us stories about his time as a professional actor. All the actors got on well – after rehearsal, we'd hang out together in the park or at the beach. Gradually, I started having a good time. At least I could spend my evenings relaxing with the crowd instead of learning my lines.

I was at home when the call came. It was the night before the play was due to open and I was doing my hair in my room. My mum called up the stairs that Jodie's dad, Duncan Parsons, was on the line. I ran downstairs and picked up the phone, my heart racing. Why was Jodie's dad calling me on the landline? Jodie always called my mobile. Perhaps something really bad had happened! Mr Parsons told me Jodie had fallen off her bike on the way home. She was going to be fine but she had injured her shoulder.

The thoughts were racing round my head. The play was opening tomorrow night and Jodie was supposed to be playing the lead! Would we cancel the play? Could someone else take the part? Poor Jodie! How was she feeling? Suddenly, I realised that Mr Parsons was still talking.

'What was that, Mr Parsons?', I asked.

'Jodie wants you to play Shirley,' he repeated.

'Me? W-w-why m-m-me?', I stammered.

'She said you knew the part,' he replied.

So, that's how I came to play Shirley. I must have somehow picked up the lines during rehearsals. I knew **them** without realising it. Everyone clapped and cheered as we took our final bow, but I'm sure Jodie would have been a better Shirley than me.

1 Why did Raquel think she was ideal for the part of Shirley?

A She was used to acting in musicals.

B She thought she matched the description of Shirley in the book.

C Shirley was the only female character in the play.

D Jodie wasn't able to sing.

2 According to the second paragraph, how do Raquel's feelings change?

A She feels even more upset about not getting the part.

B She develops feelings of jealousy towards Jodie.

C She becomes frustrated that Jodie can't learn her lines.

D She begins to accept that Jodie was right for the part.

3 Why does Raquel describe the summer in paragraph 3?

A She wants to show she was no longer disappointed about the play.

B She wants to show what a good director Matthew was.

C She wants to emphasise that Jodie was missing out on the fun.

D She wants to demonstrate that she had made new friends.

4 How did Raquel feel when she heard that Jodie's father wanted to talk to her?

A annoyed because she was busy doing her hair

B hopeful that Jodie would not be able to play Shirley

C worried that something was wrong

D scared in case he was angry with her

5 In the final paragraph, what does *them* refer to?

A the other parts in the play

B Shirley's words

C the other actors

D the audience

6 At the end of the extract, Raquel's attitude could be described as

A arrogant.

B pessimistic.

C modest.

D frustrated.

WRITING PART 1

1 Read the Writing Part 1 question and model essay. Choose from 1–3 the option that best reflects the writer's own idea.

1 celebrities' influence on teenagers
2 celebrities' wealth
3 celebrities' other responsibilities

Some celebrities are paid huge sums of money to entertain us. Do you think this is reasonable?

Notes
Write about:
1. celebrities' loss of privacy
2. celebrities without talent
3. … (your own idea)

We have all seen photos of celebrities' luxury yachts and flashy cars. The wealth of the stars is clearly visible in fashion magazines and the tabloids. In my view, **this** is totally unnecessary and creates negative values in society.

Some may say that famous people deserve their millions because their lives are no longer their own. **They** are followed everywhere by photographers. But this happens only because they are so rich. We would be less interested if they wore cheap clothes and drove ordinary cars.

Only a small proportion of well-known people actually have talent. The internet has made more people than ever recognisable and allowed them to make money from their fame. These 'fake celebrities' definitely don't deserve to be so well paid.

When young people observe the huge fortunes actors and singers have, **they** tend to undervalue ordinary jobs, such as being a nurse or a teacher. **These** used to be the ones children aspired to, but now they just want to be rich and famous.

Overall, I believe 'stars' should be paid a moderate amount of money, just like the rest of us.

---

2 The writer achieves coherence by using lexical groups. Put the words and phrases into the correct column to show which lexical groups they belong to. The first one has been done for you.

wealth   well-known   ordinary cars   teacher
celebrities   make money   huge fortunes   actors
flashy cars   recognisable   millions   famous people
well paid   the stars   rich   nurse   cheap clothes
singers

MONEY	FAME	POSSESSIONS	JOBS
wealth			

3 Read the model answer again. What do the words in bold refer to?

1 this ....
2 they ....
3 they ....
4 these ....

12 LET'S CELEBRATE

GRAMMAR

1 Look at the notices. For each one, choose the TWO sentences which match the meaning of the notice.

1

> **FESTIVAL ENTRY FEE:**
> **£5.00** – NO CHANGE GIVEN *(CARDS ACCEPTED)*

A You should have the exact money if you want to pay cash.

B It is possible to pay by card.

C It is compulsory to pay by card.

2

> STRICTLY
> OVER 18s **ONLY**
> IN THE RESTAURANT AFTER 8 pm

A Parents mustn't bring their children to the restaurant after 8 pm.

B Children are not permitted in the restaurant before 8pm.

C To eat in the restaurant after 8 pm you have to be over 18.

3

> **FESTIVAL OF FLOWERS**
> Recommended donation: £3.50 per adult

A All adults are obliged to pay £3.50.

B You ought to give a donation.

C It is not compulsory to give a donation.

4

> **FIREWORKS FORBIDDEN IN THE PARK**

A You must not take fireworks to the park.

B Bringing fireworks to the park is not essential.

C Visitors to the park are not allowed to bring fireworks with them.

5

> **DINNER INVITATION** (TIES OPTIONAL)

A It's not advisable to wear a tie.

B It's not compulsory to wear a tie.

C You don't have to wear a tie.

6

> **KEEP OFF THE GRASS**

A You do not need to walk on the grass.

B You must not walk on the grass.

C You should not walk on the grass.

2 Complete the second sentence so that it has a similar meaning to the first sentence, using the word given. Do not change the word given. You must use between two and five words.

1 That was not the right thing to do.
OUGHT
You .... that.

2 Let's climb that hill – we will have a good view of the ceremony from there.
ABLE
Let's climb that hill – we .... see the ceremony well from there.

3 We had to pay double for our tickets because we booked so late.
NEEDED
If we had booked early, we .... pay double for our tickets.

4 I managed to see all my favourite bands at the festival.
ABLE
I .... all my favourite bands at the festival.

5 It would have been better to include children's films at the film festival.
SHOULD
They .... children's films at the film festival.

6 Talking is not permitted during the main ceremony.
MUST
Visitors .... during the main ceremony.

7 Participation in the events is not compulsory.
HAVE
You .... in the events.

PUSH YOURSELF C1

Put the sentences below in the tenses shown in brackets.

1 All guests must show their invitations on the door. (FUTURE)

2 We might be able to catch the last few minutes. (PAST)

3 You can't take food into the arena. (FUTURE)

4 You should bring your identity card with you. (PAST)

5 They can book their tickets via the app. (FUTURE)

VOCABULARY

1 Use the word given in capitals at the end of some of the lines to form a word that fits in the gap in the same line.

Edinburgh Festivals	
Every year in August, Scotland's capital city plays host to two festivals: the Edinburgh International Festival and the Edinburgh Fringe. So what's the difference? To perform at the Edinburgh Festival you need an **(1)** _____ from the organisers. These are only given to **(2)** _____ musicians, singers or theatre companies. If you attend the main festival, you will have the opportunity to see an **(3)** _____ range of concerts and plays. Performers at the Fringe are not invited but they turn up **(4)** _____ . Whereas the main festival is a serious event with ballets, operas and plays, the Fringe is a **(5)** _____ mix of comedy and shows put on by amateurs. There are no formal **(6)** _____ for taking part: just come along! Every year a few **(7)** _____ will be talent-spotted at the Fringe and given the chance to join a top theatre company or orchestra. Although you rarely have to pay more than a few pounds to attend a Fringe show, it is actually more **(8)** _____ than the main Festival!	**INVITE** **EXCEPT** **IMPRESS** **REGARD** **DELIGHT** **REQUIRE** **HOPE** **PROFIT**

2 Choose a phrasal verb from the box to replace the underlined word or phrase in each sentence. Put the phrasal verb into the correct form and make any other changes that are needed.

~~look after~~	come up against	dress up	get into
go ahead	miss out on	turn down	put on

Example

Who's <u>taking care of</u> the wedding arrangements?
Who's *looking after* the wedding arrangements?

1 In my last year at school, we <u>performed</u> a Shakespeare play.

....

2 I love <u>wearing</u> sparkly costumes at the carnival each year.

....

3 When we arranged the local festival, we <u>faced</u> many obstacles.

....

4 OK, since we all think we should have Mum's 60th birthday party at Chessington Manor, we should <u>proceed</u> and book it.

....

5 If we don't get our tickets early, we might <u>lose the chance to see</u> the best bands.

....

6 After going to the festival, I really <u>started to enjoy</u> rap music.

....

7 My sister was invited to take part in the May Queen pageant but she <u>declined</u> the offer.

....

3 Complete the gaps in the text with words in the box from Unit 12.

| accessible | appeal | host | publicise | reputation |
| unique | upcoming | venues | volunteer | |

Festivals have changed a lot in recent years. Whereas in the past the **(1)** _____ was mainly to young people, they are increasingly attracting a wider range of attendees. Music festivals, in particular, had a **(2)** _____ for being uncomfortable events held in muddy fields. There is now a diverse range of **(3)** _____ , from parks and gardens to stately homes and exhibition centres. Festival organisers are more and more aware of the need for their event to be **(4)** _____ to everyone, including all age groups and people with disabilities. The improved reputation of festivals means that more places are willing to **(5)** _____ them, particularly as they are more likely to be profitable. Another boost for the popularity of festivals has come from the internet. It is now much easier and cheaper to **(6)** _____ your event to people all over the world, via social media for example. Also, the increased competitiveness of the job market means that many young people are willing to **(7)** _____ to work at festivals, just to have the experience on their CVs. In addition to the most common music-based festivals, we are seeing some **(8)** _____ festivals appear on the scene. The garlic festival on the Isle of Wight in the UK, for example, celebrates this item of food and is a fun family day out. Check on the internet or in your local newspaper to find **(9)** _____ festivals near you.

LISTENING PART 4

20 You will hear a man called Paul Fenton being interviewed about his job as a film festival organiser. For questions 1–7, choose the best answer (A, B or C).

1 According to Paul, why has a job like his become necessary?
- **A** More people want to go to specialised film festivals.
- **B** More people visit the well-known film festivals.
- **C** Film festivals have become more international.

2 What does Paul say about the Brief Encounters film festival?
- **A** It shows films relating to current issues.
- **B** It is an example of a specialist film festival.
- **C** It is a festival based in one city.

3 What advice does Paul give on choosing a type of festival?
- **A** decide whether it will be an annual event
- **B** look into different funding options
- **C** find out what local people are interested in

4 In Paul's view, why did the Fantasm festival end?
- **A** because audiences lost interest in the genre
- **B** because of a lack of films in the genre
- **C** because the organisers started to include less specialised films

5 Paul feels that most people who plan a film festival for the first time
- **A** don't have a clear idea of what they want to do.
- **B** realise it will take at least a year to plan it.
- **C** think it will take less time than it actually does.

6 Paul can give advice to new organisers on
- **A** legal, organisational and advertising issues.
- **B** deciding on the theme of the festival.
- **C** only the venues and the advertising campaign.

7 Overall, what does Paul consider the main purpose of his job?
- **A** advising on regulations relating to film festivals
- **B** offering his clients comprehensive advice
- **C** hiring the right staff on behalf of his clients

WRITING PART 2: EMAIL

1 Read this Writing Part 2 task. Below it is a sample answer written by a student called Serena. Some of the vocabulary in her answer, though, could be more interesting. Replace the <u>underlined</u> words and phrases with words and phrases from the box.

> You have received this email from your friend Nat, who is planning to visit you in your hometown.
>
> From: Nat
>
> Re: Festival
>
> Hi!
>
> As you suggested, my parents and I have managed to book our holiday to coincide with the local festival in your town. We are really excited! Could you let us know a bit about it and give us some advice on what to bring, what to wear, etc?
>
> Write your **email**.

scorching	only takes place	stunning	a bit tricky
is a massive range of	all this is accompanied by		
a blast	huge mansions		

> Hi Nat,
>
> I was really excited to get your email this morning. I thought flights might be **(1)** <u>hard</u> to get at that time, so it's great you managed to book some.
>
> To tell you something about the festival, it's called Los Patios and it **(2)** <u>is only on</u> here in Córdoba. The main thing is that you can see all the private gardens that are normally closed to the public. There **(3)** <u>are a lot of</u> **(4)** <u>beautiful</u> displays of flowers and plants in the courtyards and patios of all kinds of homes – from **(5)** <u>big houses</u> to apartments. What they have in common is that they are colourful and creative, and the owners are really proud of them. As this is the south of Spain, **(6)** <u>there's also</u> lots of eating, music and dancing, so prepare to have **(7)** <u>a good time</u>!
>
> Regarding what to bring, there are two important things: your camera – or a phone with a good camera – and walking shoes as you will be doing a lot of walking. The weather can be **(8)** <u>very hot</u> in May, so bring light cotton clothes and sun cream.
>
> See you soon!
>
> Serena

2 The email in Exercise 1 uses a good range of sentence structures and cohesive devices. Find examples of the following structures.

1 Phrases to introduce answers to the questions in the task
2 Modal auxiliary verbs
3 Adjective + preposition
4 Verb + infinitive
5 A phrase to highlight importance
6 The future continuous
7 The passive voice

13 IN FASHION, ON TREND

GRAMMAR

1 Two of the answers to each question are correct, one is not. Choose the INCORRECT answer.

1 What does your brother look like?
- **A** He's tall with curly brown hair.
- **B** He looks a bit like me.
- **C** He looks like handsome.

2 What do you feel like doing this evening?
- **A** I like playing football.
- **B** I feel like going out for a nice meal.
- **C** I'm not sure. What do you want to do?

3 What does James do?
- **A** He works as an assistant to the managing director.
- **B** He's an accounts manager.
- **C** He works like a fashion designer.

4 What is your new boss like?
- **A** She's really nice – kind and very funny.
- **B** I don't like her. She treats me as an idiot.
- **C** Awful. She treats me like her servant.

5 What does his new single sound like?
- **A** It sounds brilliant.
- **B** It sounds like fantastic.
- **C** It sounds a bit like his early songs.

2 Complete the second sentence so that it has a similar meaning to the first sentence, using the word given. Do not change the form of the word given. Use between two and five words.

1 My brother is a software engineer for a big IT firm.
WORKS
My brother _____ for a big IT firm.

2 My aunt thinks that I am a child. It's so annoying.
TREATS
My aunt _____ child. It's so annoying.

3 My sister and I are so alike. People think we're twins.
JUST
My sister _____ me. People think we're twins.

4 I can tell that you've had a lot of fun today.
LOOKS
It _____ you've had a lot of fun today.

5 They heard what they thought was a loud cheer coming from inside the building.
SOUNDED
They heard _____ a loud cheer coming from inside the building.

3 Do the pairs of sentences have similar or different meanings? Write S (similar) or D (different).

1 You shouldn't have bought those jeans without trying them on.
It's good that you tried on those jeans before you bought them.

2 I needn't have tried on so many dresses as I ended up buying the first one I tried.
I wasted my time trying on more dresses after I'd found the right one.

3 I wouldn't have bought a car from that dealer if I'd read the online reviews.
The dealer had bad reviews online but I didn't see them until after I'd bought the car.

4 You didn't really need to wear a suit to that event but you looked good.
The event required men to wear suits and you looked good in the one you wore.

5 What you should have done was to have talked to the manager immediately.
You didn't talk to the manager immediately but that would have been the right thing to do.

6 Sabrina needn't have ordered so many flowers – one bunch would have been enough.
Sabrina ordered only one bunch of flowers because that was all she needed.

VOCABULARY

1 Complete each sentence with a word you learned in Unit 13. The first letter has been given for each gap.

1 I think the most expensive p_____ _____ I've ever made was when I bought a brand new car.

2 I've never actually won an online a_____ _____ _____. Once the price goes too high, I give up.

3 I got an amazing b_____ _____ _____ last week – a new camera at half price!

4 I think that most c_____ _____ shop for clothes online rather than going into shops.

5 I always go on a big shopping s_____ as soon as I get paid every month.

6 Julia Smith is a famous v_____ _____ who always has some really useful shopping tips when I watch her videos online.

7 I have loads of old o_____ _____ that don't fit me any more so I'm going to donate them to charity.

8 My country i_____ _____ a lot of fruit and vegetables from abroad which means you can buy most things all year round.

9 The company has hired a famous basketball player for its new marketing c_____ _____ _____.

10 I used to work in the fashion i_____ _____ before setting up my own company.

2 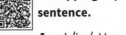 21 Listen to two friends, Marc and Julia, talking about a shopping trip. Choose the correct option for each sentence.

1 *Julia / Marc* is planning to spend some money.

2 Julia and Marc *have been / have never been* shopping together before.

3 Marc has *more / less* money than usual.

4 The last time he went shopping, Marc *didn't buy much / spent too much*.

5 Julia *seems to know / doesn't seem to know* Marc very well.

3 21 Listen again and complete the phrases.

1 … maybe do a little _____ .

2 … I was thinking of hunting out a few _____ .

3 … a little look around the shops always turns into a _____ .

4 I'm on a very tight _____ at the moment.

5 I know how you love your _____ .

6 … if you're willing to _____ a bit.

7 … I'm sure you're not going to come home _____ .

8 … but I'm not going to _____ like I did last time.

PUSH YOURSELF C1

Rearrange the words to form sentences.

1 spending / it / too / case / a / money / more / ~~Isn't~~ / people / of / much
Isn't _____ ?

2 like / it / don't / that / see / I / just / ~~I'm~~ / afraid
I'm _____ .

3 always / case / not / ~~Actually,~~ / the / that's
Actually, _____ .

4 have / agree / to / ~~I~~ / we'll / guess / to / disagree / just
I _____ .

5 don't / eye / that / eye / see / we / ~~I~~ / to / it's / think / clear
I _____ .

6 see / not / it / way / quite / ~~That's~~ / the / I
That's _____ .

READING AND USE OF ENGLISH PART 4

For questions 1–6, complete the second sentence so that it has a similar meaning to the first sentence, using the word given. Do not change the word given. You must use between two and five words. Here is an example (0).

Example

0 Kathy's clothes are always more fashionable than Jackson's.

AS

Jackson's clothes *are never as fashionable as* Kathy's.

1 The student copied the idea from a famous designer but he didn't get caught.

AWAY

The student .... the idea from a famous designer.

2 Children should always obey their parents.

AS

Children should always .... them.

3 Do you want to go to that new shopping centre today?

FEEL

Do you .... that new shopping centre today?

4 Sadly, I don't know much about the new design proposal.

UNFAMILIAR

Sadly, ... the new design proposal.

5 Seeing John at the party was a surprise.

EXPECT

I .... John at the party.

6 You always force me into watching football every weekend!

MAKE

You always .... football every weekend!

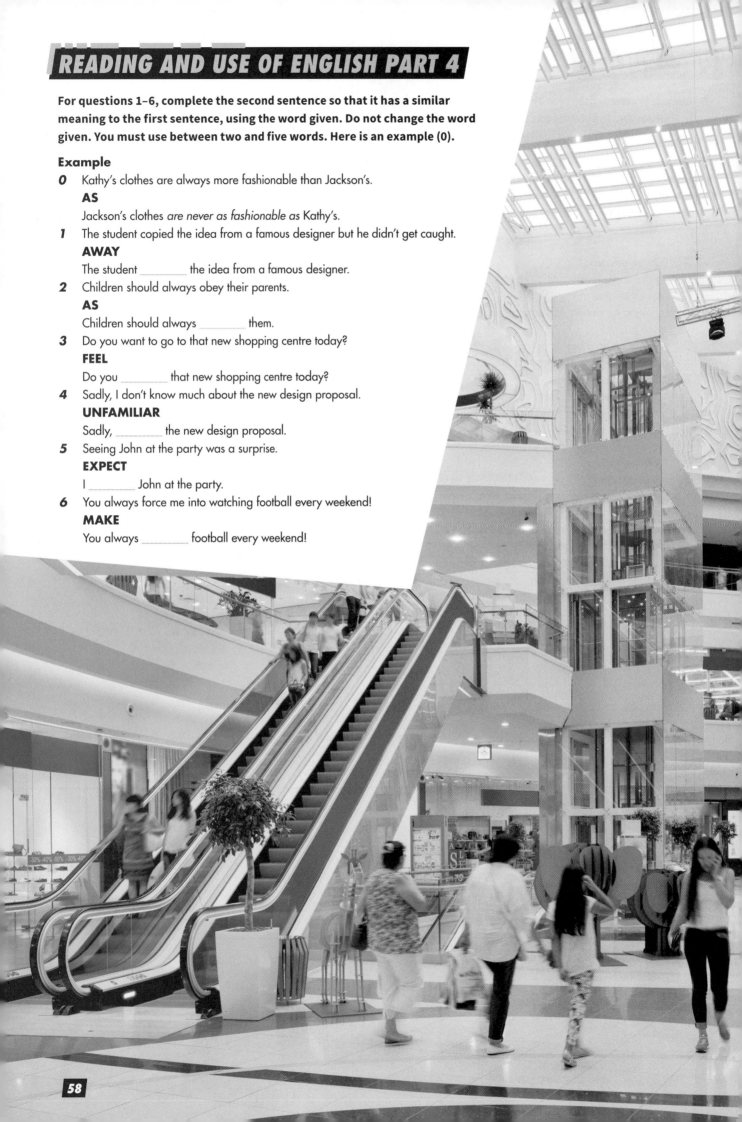

SPEAKING PART 2

1 **22 Look at the Part 2 Speaking task below. Listen to a student called Hamid doing the task. Choose the correct options, A or B.**

Why do you think the people are enjoying shopping in these situations?

1 **A** Hamid starts by talking about Picture 1.
   B Hamid starts with ideas that relate to both pictures.
2 **A** Hamid then moves on to talk about each picture individually.
   B Hamid continues to talk about both pictures.
3 **A** Hamid spends about the same amount of time on each picture.
   B Hamid talks more about Picture 1 than about Picture 2.
4 **A** Hamid mostly just describes what he can see in the photos.
   B Hamid uses modals to suggest ideas related to the photos.
5 **A** Hamid gives his opinion of the markets.
   B Hamid sticks to the facts.
6 **A** He ends by talking about Picture 2.
   B He ends with his opinion of what the markets have in common.

2  **22 Listen again. Complete the sentences with the exact words Hamid uses.**

1 I think they are both enjoying themselves because they _____ in a hurry at all.
2 … the lady is choosing some food – it _____ fruit.
3 That's _____ one reason why she's enjoying it.
4 … I think the food _____ very fresh …
5 … it _____ locally grown and organic.
6 The things on sale _____ second hand …
7 … or _____ antiques.
8 … so that _____ why she looks happy.

14 NOT JUST 9–5

GRAMMAR

1 Rewrite the sentences to make them more emphatic, using the words in brackets.

Example
You need to log on to our website and complete the application form. (What)

What you need to do is log on to our website and complete the application form.

1 You must not reveal the plans for the new products to anyone. (Under no circumstances)
2 You realise how easy student life is when you start working full-time. (It's only)
3 I feel that most companies still don't give employees enough time off. (What)
4 Isla runs her own company and works as a volunteer at the local hospital. (Not only, but also)
5 This is the first time I've worked with such annoying people! (Never)
6 I find it frustrating that you can only get a job if you already have experience. (What)

2 Choose the correct option to complete the sentences.

1 I *have known / have been knowing* Jessica for almost five years.
2 I avoid *to eat / eating* food which contains nuts because I'm allergic.
3 I've been working at the hospital for six months but I'm still *being / getting* used to the early starts.
4 *Provided / Unless* he passes his final exam, Simon will start university in the autumn.
5 There's been a noticeable drop in the number of tourists visiting the town which has caused *many / much* of the restaurants there to close.
6 We *didn't even finish / hadn't even finished* our starters when, suddenly, the main course turned up.
7 They *prevented / warned* us against travelling on the roads due to the poor weather conditions.
8 I really regret not *to study / studying* computer programming at school as it's such a useful skill to have nowadays.
9 The restaurant's always fully booked. The food there *can't / must* be really good.
10 It doesn't look like the engineers *will have fixed / will be fixing* the issue in time for the start of the concert.
11 The tour guide will let us *join / to join* the tour, provided we pay the full amount in advance.
12 The manager *denied / refused* to give me a refund even though I had a receipt.
13 It isn't *compulsory / permitted* to make a donation but you can if you want to.
14 I *needn't have eaten / shouldn't have eaten* that last piece of cake. I feel really sick now.
15 Under no circumstances *you must / must you* speak during the exam.

VOCABULARY

1 🔊 **23 Listen to six people talking about their jobs. For each speaker, choose a job from the box.**

financial advisor   pilot   freelance consultant
police officer   children's entertainer
machine operator   property developer
tax adviser   doctor   pharmacist
air traffic controller

Speaker 1 ....
Speaker 2 ....
Speaker 3 ....
Speaker 4 ....
Speaker 5 ....
Speaker 6 ....

2 **Complete each gap with a word from the box. There are two words you do not need.**

redundant   freelance
expenses   sack   employed
application   notice
promotion   vacancy   apply

1. I'm thinking of going .... as I like the idea of being my own boss.
2. I am writing to submit my .... for the job of receptionist.
3. It's a good idea to find another job before you hand in your ....
4. The car factory had to make a quarter of the workforce .... because there wasn't enough work.
5. Our company has very strict rules about how much you can claim on .... when you go on a business trip.
6. You will need to work long hours if you want to get a ....
7. It's not as easy as it used to be to give someone the .... as there are laws to protect workers.
8. I would love to work for Greyson's, but they don't have a .... at the moment.

3 **Match each sentence (1 – 8) with the sentence that has a similar meaning (A–H).**

1. Could you possibly set it up?
2. The comment has now been taken down from the website.
3. I haven't got round to analysing the problem yet.
4. Why don't you run this report by the consultant?
5. They've put the meeting back by a week.
6. Let me get back to you later today.
7. The CEO is looking into expanding the company.
8. We need to cut back on the amount we spend on taxis and flights.

A. I haven't had time to examine the issue.
B. It's vital that we reduce our travel costs.
C. We have removed the message from the page.
D. It might be worth asking him to look at it.
E. The head of the organisation wants to increase the size of the company.
F. I'll let you know this afternoon.
G. It has been moved to a later date.
H. It would be great if you could organise it.

PUSH YOURSELF C1

Write a word or words for each definition. The first letter of each one has been given to help you.

1. A kind of training session which includes activities.
   w............................

2. The person with the same position in another company or country.
   c............................

3. A field of work which involves placing people in jobs.
   r............................

4. Give up a job or position, especially an important one.
   s............................ d............................

5. The amount of money taken by a business in a particular period.
   t............................

6. A person who is addicted to work.
   w............................

7. Another word for getting sacked.
   d............................

8. The amount of work that needs to be done.
   w............................

24 **You will hear a woman called Maya talking about her job as a florist. For questions 1–10, complete the sentences with a word or short phrase.**

1 Maya originally studied _____ .
2 Maya was employed by other people for eight years before setting up her own _____ .
3 Maya says she was fortunate because her _____ provided a place for her to run her business.
4 Some people buy flowers to give to someone who is _____ from the workplace.
5 Maya is particularly happy when she does flowers for couples who are celebrating their _____ wedding anniversaries.
6 Maya explains that it can sometimes be difficult to arrange flowers for _____ because they have very high expectations.
7 The floristry trade has been impacted by changes to the _____ .
8 Maya believes that everyone can be _____ if they try hard enough.
9 Maya says that florists should be _____ as some of their customers are buying flowers to say sorry to someone.
10 Florists have to compete with _____ for business.

1 Read the Writing Part 2 task and the email written by a student called Gonzalo. Find and correct the <u>eight</u> spelling mistakes.

You see this advert for volunteers to work on projects abroad.

> **Volunteer with Help Abroad**
> Would you like to use your holidays to develop your skills, experience a new culture and meet people from all over the world? If so, our volunteering opportunities overseas could be for you. Choose from working on a farm, helping to build a school, or teaching English to children. We have opportunities in South America, Africa and Asia.
> Apply by email to John Patton at johnp@helpabroad.co.uk, saying why you want to volunteer with Help Abroad. Please tell us the kind of work you are interested in, the skills and personal qualities you have that make you suitable, and your preferred location.

Write your **letter**.

Dear Mr Patton,

I am writing to express my intarest in volunteering for Help Abroad. I am committed to improving life for people in the developing world and your organisation would give me an excellent oppertunity to do that.

I am interested mainly in construction work. I have done some bricklaying with my uncle during my school holidays and he has taught me some basic building skils. I am planning to study arcitecture at university from next October and have a special interest in enviromentally-friendly design. I think this would make me a strong candidate for the school-building projec.

I am a very practical kind of person who likes to take a hands-on approach to whatever I do. I am also physically fit, which I feel would help with the work I have chosen. I am wiling to go to any location where my skills are needed. However, as a Spanish speaker, I might be of greatest use in South America.

I am availible at any time to discuss this opportunity further.

Yours sincerely

Gonzalo Muñoz

---

2 The following comments were made by the examiner about Gonzalo's email. Match each one with one of the four marking criteria.

> Content   Communicative achievement
> Organisation   Language

1 The candidate uses collocation appropriately (*special interest, environmentally-friendly, hands-on approach*).

2 The email begins and ends with appropriate conventions of formal writing (*Dear Mr, I am writing to, Yours sincerely*).

3 Linking expressions are used to good effect (*also, however*). The writing avoids repetition through referencing (*this would make me*) and paraphrase (*construction work … the work I have chosen*).

4 All parts of the email relate to the task; the candidate has clearly explained what type of work he wants to do and the skills and personal qualities he could bring to the project.

5 Topic-specific vocabulary is used (*developing world, bricklaying, building skills*).

6 The email is appropriately formal throughout.

7 There is a good range of sentence structure (relative clauses, modals, verb patterns).

8 Paragraphs are well organised and begin in a variety of ways.

ACKNOWLEDGEMENTS

The authors and publishers acknowledge the following sources of copyright material and are grateful for the permissions granted. While every effort has been made, it has not always been possible to identify the sources of all the material used, or to trace all copyright holders. If any omissions are brought to our notice, we will be happy to include the appropriate acknowledgements on reprinting and in the next update to the digital edition, as applicable.

Key: UST = Unit Starter, U = Unit

Text
U3: Portfolio School for the text about the school. Copyright © Portfolio School. Reproduced with kind permission.

Photography
All the images are sourced from Getty Images.

UST: Klaus Vedfelt/DigitalVision; SolStock/iStock/Getty Images Plus; Tony Anderson/Taxi; **U1:** Cultura RM Exclusive/Alan Graf; Felix Man/Stringer/Picture Post; Mike Harrington/DigitalVision; **U2:** Caiaimage/Robert Daly; FatCamera/E+; **U3:** Ariel Skelley/DigitalVision; Portra/DigitalVision; **U4:** Andrew TB Tan/Moment; levente bodo/Moment; Tais Policanti/Momen; **U5:** Tim Robberts/The Image Bank; Anthony Harvie/Stone; Ravindra Bhor/iStock/Getty Images Plus; Tetra Images; **U6:** Gary Vestal/Photographer's Choice; moodboard/Brand X Pictures; Chris Cheadle/All Canada Photos; **U7:** mikroman6/Moment; David Malan/Photographer's Choice; Mike Kemp; **U8:** Indeed; Dong Wenjie/Moment; Dennis Macdonald/Photographer's Choice RF; **U9:** Caiaimage/Sam Edwards; Hero Images; Vlad Fishman/Moment; Ventura Carmona/Moment; **U10:** momentimages; Hero Images; **U11:** Westend61; Mike Kemp/Blend Images; Caiaimage/Martin Barraud; **U12:** Gpointstudio/Image Source; NLink/iStock/Getty Images Plus; **U13:** JAG IMAGES/Cultura; Vostok/Moment; Hoxton/Tom Merton; asiseeit/E+; **U14:** kali9/E+; Alys Tomlinson/Cultura; Ariel Skelley/DigitalVision.

Front cover photography by Supawat Punnanon/EyeEm; Patrick Foto; fStop Images-Caspar Benson; art2002; Alexander Spatari; primeimages.

Illustrations
Derren Toussaint (In the style of Steven Johnson).

Audio
Produced by Creative Listening and recorded at Tileyard Studios, London.

Page make up
EMC Design Ltd